D0896783

How They Found Christ

in their own words

— Expanded Edition —

Edited by
Bill Freeman

Ministry
Publications
Scottsdale, Arizona

First Edition 1983
Second Edition, Expanded 1998

Library of Congress Catalog
Card Number: 97-78492

ISBN 0-914271-94-6

Ministry Publications
P.O. Box 12222
Scottsdale, Arizona 85267
(602) 948-4050 / (800) 573-4105
E-mail: MinWord12@aol.com

Printed in the United States of America

Contents

Preface

This book brings together the personal testimonies of some of God's servants from the past to let them tell in their own words *How They Found Christ.* Nothing is more touching than to hear exactly what was taking place at the time a person found Christ. What was the state of their mind? What were their doubts? What problems were they facing? What were their religious concepts? How did they actually find Christ? What happened within them when they experienced Christ?

You may feel that you are the only one who is having doubts and inner conflicts over your relationship with God. You may even feel hopeless about finding Christ because of these problems, doubts, and concepts. If this is your case, reading this book can be the turning point in your life.

The various conditions that existed in the lives of the sixteen men and women presented in this book are the same that exist in our lives today. These conditions were present with them at the time they found Christ and may be summarized as follows: (1) Augustine — *a sinful life,* (2) Martin Luther — *a troubled conscience,* (3) John Calvin — *an arrested life,* (4) John Bunyan — *mental conflict,* (5) Madame Guyon — *a searching heart,* (6) John Wesley — *a defeated life,* (7) Jonathan Edwards

— *miserable seeking,* (8) George Whitefield — *a religious life,* (9) Charles Finney — *a proud heart,* (10) George Müller — *indifference toward God,* (11) Andrew Murray — *an impacted life,* (12) Hannah W. Smith — *a discovery of God,* (13) Hudson Taylor — *ignorance of the gospel,* (14) Charles Spurgeon — *a seeking heart,* (15) A. B. Simpson — *a desperate situation,* and (16) Watchman Nee — *a successful life.*

Their testimonies illustrate the many different conditions in which God's grace works to lead men's hearts to Christ. At the conclusion of each testimony, a brief explanation is given to apply from the Word of God how *you* can find Christ. And the last chapter shows you how you can have the assurance that you have found Him. May the Holy Spirit guide you into the reality of finding Christ as you enjoy the testimonies in this book.

—Bill Freeman
February 1998

S cripture quotations are taken from a combination of translations including *The New King
James Version,*[†] *The King James Version, The
New American Standard Version,*[§] etc. Minor
changes have been made in the various versions
from time to time to give a better rendering of the
Hebrew and Greek texts.

Throughout the Scripture quotations, words
are italicized for added emphasis.

In some of the testimonies, antiquated spell-
ing, punctuation, or wording has been updated for
the sake of the reader's understanding.

---

1 Aurelius Augustine

• A Sinful Life •

"Instantly, as the sentence ended…all the gloom of doubt vanished away."

(354-430)

*A*ugustine's life and ministry has left an indelible mark on the history of the church. He was an able defender of the Christian faith whose writings were deeply founded in personal experience.

Augustine was a son of the many prayers of his mother, Monica. She had the greatest impact upon his life in the years leading up to his dynamic experience of salvation. Part of that impact was in her relating a vision to Augustine that revealed he would one day be saved in answer to her prayers.

As a youth Augustine lived a checkered life. He dabbled in rhetoric, theater, philosophy, and heresy. At the same time, he lived a sinful life with one mistress and then another. The inability within himself to give up his lust and sinful way of life eventually became the focal point of his struggle that led him to find Christ.

In her deep desire to win Augustine to the Lord, his mother would often entreat others with tears to plead with him. One such person was a faithful bishop, who declined because he felt Augustine was not yet in a state to hear the gospel. The bishop left her with these words: "Leave him there, and only pray to God for him; he will discover by reading what is his error, and how great his impiety. Go, live so; it cannot be that the son of those tears will perish."

While his mother was praying for him, Augustine was coming under the powerful preaching of Ambrose in Milan. Concerning him Augustine said, "I was led to him unknowingly by God, that I might knowingly be led to God by him." The main verse that was on the lips of Ambrose in those days was 2 Corinthians 3:6, "The letter kills, but the Spirit gives life." This made a deep impression upon Augustine.

At this juncture in his life, he was also deeply touched by hearing the testimony of Victorinus, a teacher of rhetoric whom Augustine admired. Victorinus had found Christ and taken a bold stand to forsake the ways of the world. A friend of Augustine's related Victorinus's testimony to him, upon which Augustine said,

I was on fire to imitate him. By his choice to give up his school of rhetoric for the sake of Christ, he seemed to me not only courageous but actually fortunate, because it gave him the opportunity to devote himself wholly to You.‡ I longed for the same opportunity, but I was bound, not with the iron of another's chains, but by my own iron will. The enemy held my will, and made a chain of it and bound me. For from a perverse will lust was born, and by giving into lust a habit was created, and when this habit was not resisted it became a necessity. These were like links hanging one on another — which is why I have called it a chain — and their hard bondage held me. ¹

It was in this condition of sinful gloom that God came to Augustine through His Word to set him free. His own words, from his confessions to the Lord, bear clear testimony to the grace of God operating in and over him to lead him to the dynamic answer to all of his mother's tears and prayers. Here he describes the torment he was passing through due to the deep conviction of sin:

I WAS SICK AT HEART and in torment, accusing myself much more bitterly than usual. I twisted and turned in my chain of bondage in the hope that it might be completely broken. For what held me was so small a thing! But it still held me. And You‡ put pressure on the secret places of my soul, O Lord, and in Your severe

‡ Augustine wrote his *Confessions* in the form of a conversation with the Lord.

mercy did not leave me to myself. You redoubled the scourges of fear and shame so that I would not give in again to my lust. The harshness of Your mercy was there lest that small remaining tie to my sinful life not be broken, but recover strength once again and bind me even closer than before.

I kept saying within myself, "Let it be done now, let it be done now," and by just speaking these words I had begun to move toward a firm decision to trust Christ for my salvation. I almost made it, yet I did not quite make it. But I did not fall back into my former state of bondage to sin, but stood aside for a moment to get my breath. And I tried again and I was almost there, and now I could almost touch Christ and hold Him. Yet I was not quite there. I did not touch or hold Him, because I still hesitated to die to sin and death, and live to life in Christ. The worse condition of habitual sin had grown more powerful in me than the better condition of freedom from sin which I had not tried. And the closer the time drew near in which I was to become different, the greater the horror of it struck me. But it did not force me utterly back or turn me utterly away, but held me in suspense between two states — bondage and freedom.

It was my old mistresses, the very toys of toys, and vanities of vanities, that held me back, tugging at my garment of flesh and murmuring softly, "Are you going to part with us?" and, "From this moment will we not be with you, now or forever?" and, "From this moment will you not be allowed to do 'this or that,' now or forever?" What were they suggesting to me by the phrase, "this or that"? What were they suggesting to me, O my God? Let Your mercy turn it away from the soul of Your servant. What impurities did they suggest! What shame! But by now I could hardly hear them, because they no longer openly opposed me face to face, but were softly muttering behind my back. As I tried to depart, they insidiously tugged at my cloak to make me look back at my old life. And they delayed me, so that I hesitated to break loose and shake myself free from them and leap over to the place to which I was called — for an unruly habit kept saying to me, "Do you think you can live without them?"

But by this time its voice was growing fainter. Then in the direction toward which I had turned my face and was trembling in fear to go, I could see the chaste dignity of Continence,* serene and happy but not in an evil way. She entreated me in an honorable way to come to her and not doubt, stretching forth her holy hands to receive and embrace me, hands full of a multitude of good examples. With her I saw so many men and women, a multitude of youth and of every age, gray widows and women grown old in virginity, and in all of them Continence herself, not

---

* "Continence" refers to morality and self-restraint, spoken of here by Augustine in a personified way.

barren but the fruitful mother of children of joys, by You, O Lord, her Spouse. And she was smiling at me with an encouraging smile, as if to say, "Can you not do what these men and women have done? Or could they have done such in themselves, and not in the Lord their God? The Lord their God gave me to them. Why do you stand in your own strength, and so do not stand at all? Cast yourself upon Him without a care. He will not withdraw Himself and let you fall. Cast yourself without fear, for He will receive you and heal you."

Yet I was still ashamed because I could still hear the murmuring of those vanities, and I was still hesitant and hanging back. And again Continence seemed to say, "Become deaf to those unclean members of yours upon the earth, that they may be put to death. They tell you of delights, but not of such delights as the law of the Lord your God tells." This was the controversy raging in my heart, a controversy of self against self. And my dear friend Alypius stayed by my side and waited in silence to see the outcome of such agitation as he had never seen in me.

Now when deep reflection and scrutiny had drawn up all my vileness from the secret depths of my soul and had heaped it up before the eyes of my heart, a mighty storm arose in me, bringing a mighty downpour of tears. I then withdrew from Alypius so that I might give way to my tears and griefs, for it seemed to me that solitude was more suitable for weeping. I went far enough from him so that his presence would not be a restraint to me. This was how I felt at the time, and he realized it.

Alypius was sensitive to my condition, for I suppose I had said something and the sound of my voice was heavy with tears. When I left him he remained where we had been sitting, still in utter amazement. I flung myself down under a certain fig tree and no longer tried to stop my tears, which poured forth from my eyes in a flood, an acceptable sacrifice to You (1 Pet. 2:5). And I said words to this effect: "And You, O Lord, how long? How long, O Lord? Will You be angry forever? Do not remember our former sins" (Psa. 6:3; 79:5, 8). For I felt that I was still in their grip. And I sent up these sorrowful cries, "How long, how long shall I go on saying tomorrow, and again tomorrow? Why not now, why not have an end to my uncleanness this very hour?"

I was saying these things and weeping in the most bitter sorrow of my heart, when suddenly I heard a voice from a neighboring house, a boy's voice or a girl's voice, I do not know, but it was a sort of sing-song, repeated again and again, "Take up and read, take up and read." I stopped weeping and immediately began most earnestly to think whether it was common for children to sing these words in any kind of game, but I could not remember ever hearing anything like it. So, holding back the flood of my tears I rose to my feet, for I could not help thinking that this was a divine command to pick up the book and read the first passage I opened to. For I had heard about Anthony, that coming in during the reading of the Gospel, he received the admonition, as if what was being read was spoken directly to him: "Go and sell what you have, and give to the poor, and you shall have treasure in heaven; and come and follow Me" (Matt. 19:21). By this experience he was immediately converted to You.

Eagerly then I returned to the place where Alypius was sitting, for I had put down the apostle's book there when I arose. I seized it, opened it, and in silence read the passage on which my eyes first fell: "Not in rioting and drunkenness, not in fornication and impurities, not in strife and envying. But put on the Lord Jesus Christ, and make no provision for the flesh, to fulfill the lusts thereof" (Rom. 13:13-14). I had no desire to read any further, and no need to. For instantly, as the sentence ended, there was infused into my heart something like the light of full certainty, and all the gloom of doubt vanished away.

Then closing the book, and putting my finger or something else in it for a marker, in complete calm I told Alypius everything. And he in turn told me what had been going on in him, which I knew nothing about. He asked to see what I had read. I showed him, and he looked on even further than I had read. I did not know what followed, but it was this: "Receive one who is weak in the faith" (Rom. 14:1). He applied this to himself and told me so. And he was strengthened by this admonition, and by exercising his good resolution and purpose — all very much in keeping with his character, for in these matters he had been much, much better than I — he joined me in full commitment without any hesitation or wavering.

Then we went inside to my mother and told her. She was filled with great joy. We explained to her how it had occurred — and she rejoiced triumphantly, and she blessed You, who are "able to do exceedingly abundantly above all that we ask or think" (Eph. 3:20). For she saw that You had given her far more than she had ever asked for with all her pitiful weeping. For You converted me to Yourself in such a way that I no longer sought a wife or any other of this world's hopes. I now stood firm upon that same rule of faith which, so many years before, You had shown her in a vision about me. You changed her mourning into joy, far richer than she had dared to desire, and much dearer and purer than the desire she used to cherish of having grandchildren of my flesh.[2]

◆

Like Augustine, you may be struggling with a sinful life. You may even be, right now, in the middle of hearing two voices speaking within you. One says, "Open to Christ now," but the other says, "No, not now, wait for another day." You should realize that the Bible speaks of these kinds of ambivalent feelings in people who are on the brink of receiving Christ. In Acts 26:14 the Lord identified for Paul his confused feelings by saying, "It is hard for you to kick against the goads." Addressing this very conflict, 2 Corinthians 6:2 declares, "Behold, *now* is the acceptable time; behold, *now* is the day of salvation."

It is not a matter of waiting for another day, thinking that *you* have to "clean up" your life before you can come to Christ. No, just as you are this moment, in the midst of fightings without and fears within, Christ will come into you and not only forgive you, but change you from within and give you a new heart.

This new heart is seen in the life of Augustine immediately after he found the Lord. The English minister F. B. Meyer tells one of his favorite stories related to the instant change in Augustine's life:

> Augustine was swept as by a mighty current between two women, his mother, Monica, a saintly woman, and another woman, who had fascinated him almost to damnation. His life hovered between these two just as your life hovers between Christ and Satan. Sometimes Monica attracted him heavenward, and then the evil influence of the other woman dragged him to the very pit of the abyss. The conflict was long and terrible, and Augustine was like a chip upon the tide, swept backward and forward. [3]

But when the Lord shined into Augustine's heart through the words in Romans 13:14 — "Put on the Lord Jesus Christ" — everything changed. F. B. Meyer continues to describe what happened to Augustine:

> Instantly he arose. He had made his decision. He had counted the cost. He told his friend Alypius, and they went and told Monica, and Monica was glad.
>
> The next day he went down the main street of Carthage. As he did so, he met the woman who had been the fascination of his soul for evil. As he met her, she said:
>
> "Augustine, it is I!"
>
> He said, "But, it is not I," and passed her and was saved. [4]

Ambrose relates this same story in one of his writings, giving a few more details of Augustine's encounter with his former mistress:

> One day meeting his old favorite and not speaking to her, she, being surprised and supposing that he had not recognized her, said, when they met again, "It is I." "But," was his answer, "I am not the former I." [5]

By opening up to Christ, your "old I" will become a "new I," and you can say with Paul in 2 Corinthians 5:17, "If anyone is in Christ, he is a new creation; old things have passed away; behold, all things have become new."

2 Martin Luther

· A Troubled Conscience ·

"I felt myself to be reborn and to have gone through open doors into paradise."

(1483-1546)

From the day he first saw into the meaning of the statement "the just shall live by faith" until now, the reverberations of Martin Luther's revelation of justification by faith have greatly impacted the church. The dynamic of Luther's salvation experience was a combination of things: his being a sensitive and devoted Augustinian monk with a troubled conscience, his observations of the corruption of the papal system, the influence of the mystic writers upon him, and his careful examination of the precise meaning of "righteousness" and "justification" in the book of Romans.

By the time Luther saw that justification was by faith alone, and not by works, he had virtually exhausted every possible means of saving himself. He had fasted, prayed, and gone on pilgrimages. He had confessed his sins over and over again to the point that his Augustinian vicar, Johann von Staupitz, said to him, "Look here, if you expect Christ to forgive you, come in with something to forgive — murder, blasphemy, adultery — instead of all these minor offenses." [1]

Luther's troubled conscience was pained over the slightest movement within him, and according to Staupitz, he seemed to thrive on his inward torment. Nevertheless, Luther's deep turmoil was preparing him to find a Christ that he had never known before. "The righteousness of God" became a revelation, not of an angry, judging God, but of the way God makes men righteous — through Christ dying on the cross, and by simple faith in that fact. Luther's own words tell the story of this far-reaching discovery:

I GREATLY LONGED to understand Paul in his letter to the Romans. Nothing stood in the way but that one expression, "the righteousness of God." I took it to mean that righteousness in which God is just and deals righteously in punishing the unjust. My inner condition was that, although an impeccable monk, I stood before God as a sinner troubled in conscience, and I had no confidence that my merit would appease Him. Therefore I did not love a righteous and angry God, but rather hated and murmured against Him. Yet I clung to the dear Paul and had a great yearning to know what he meant.

Finally, after days and nights of wrestling with the difficulty, God had mercy on me, and I saw the connection between the righteousness of God and the statement "the just shall live by his faith." Then I understood that the righteousness of God is that righteousness by which, through grace and sheer mercy, God justifies us through faith. Then I felt myself to be reborn and to have gone through open doors into paradise. The whole of Scripture took on a new meaning. Before, the "the righteousness of God" had filled me with hate, but now it became to me inexpressibly sweet in greater love. This passage of Paul's became to me a gate to heaven.[2]

Instantly all Scripture looked different to me. I passed through the Holy Scriptures, so far as I was able to recall them from memory, and gathered a similar sense from other expressions: the "work of God" is that which God works in us; the "strength of God" is that through which He makes us strong; the "wisdom of God" is that through which He makes us wise; and the "power of God," the "blessing of God," and the "honor of God" are expressions used in the same way. Thus, as intensely as I had formerly hated the expression "righteousness of God," I now loved and praised it as the sweetest of concepts. And so this passage of Paul's actually was the doorway of paradise to me.

These words, "the just" and "righteousness," were lightning and thunder in my conscience under the papacy, and merely hearing them mentioned terrified me. In this tower, in which there was a special place for the monks, I once meditated on these words: "The just lives by faith" (Hab. 2:4), and "the righteousness of God" (Rom. 1:17). Then it suddenly came to my mind: If we are to live righteously because of righteousness by faith, and this righteousness of God is intended to save everyone who believes, it follows that righteousness is by faith, and life by righteousness. And my conscience and spirit were lifted up, and I was made certain that it is the righteousness of God which justifies and saves us. And immediately these words became sweet and delightful words to me. These things the Holy Spirit taught me in this tower.

This most excellent righteousness — the righteousness of faith — which God imputes to us through Christ, without our works, is neither a civil nor a ceremonial righteousness nor one of the divine Law nor one concerned with our works. This righteousness is totally different, that is, a merely passive righteousness, just as those mentioned above are active righteousnesses. For in this righteousness we do nothing, nor do we have anything to give to God. We only receive and allow Another to work within us, that is to say, God. That is why this righteousness of faith, or this Christian righteousness, may be called a passive righteousness.

This is the righteousness shrouded in mystery (Col. 1:26), a righteousness which the world does not understand, and not only so, but one which even Christians do not sufficiently grasp and which they find difficult to cling to in times of temptation. This is why we must constantly drill it and stress it without ceasing. And he who does not grasp it and cling to it in the middle of afflictions and the terrors of conscience cannot hold his own; for besides this passive righteousness there is no other comfort of conscience so firm and certain.

All works, however holy they may be, are completely excluded and put aside as being necessary for salvation. If a good work can save a man, then apples and pears can also save him! Christian righteousness is not a righteousness that is within us and clings to us, as a quality or virtue does. It is not something that is found to be part of us or something that is felt by us. But it is a foreign righteousness entirely outside of us, namely, Christ Himself is our essential Righteousness and complete Satisfaction (1 Cor. 1:30).

In order to better grasp this matter, I am in the habit of imagining that there is no quality in my heart called faith or love. Instead, I put Christ in its place and say, "This is my Righteousness." I do this in order to free myself from looking to the Law for righteousness or from regarding this Christ as merely a Teacher or Giver of knowledge. Rather, I want Him to be my Gift and my Doctrine in His own Person, so that I have everything in Him, just as He says, "I am the Way" (John 14:6). He does not say, "I give you the way," as if He were working and giving me this way while He Himself is standing outside of me. He must be, remain, live, and speak *in* me, as Paul says, "That we might be the righteousness of God in Him," not in the love and gifts that follow (2 Cor. 5:21). [3]

If you have a true faith that Christ is your Savior, then at once you have a gracious God, for faith leads you in and opens up God's heart and will, that you should see pure grace and overflowing love. This it is to behold God in faith that you should look upon His fatherly, friendly heart, in which there is no anger or ungraciousness. He who sees God as angry does not see Him rightly but looks only on a curtain, as if a dark cloud had been drawn across His face. [4]

Our foundation and firm anchor-hold must always be Christ as our only perfect righteousness. If we have nothing in which we may trust, yet these three things, faith, hope, and love do remain (1 Cor. 13:13). Therefore we must always believe and hope; we must always take hold of Christ as the source and fountain of our righteousness. He who believes in Him shall not be ashamed. At the same time, we must labor to be outwardly righteous also, that is, not to consent to the flesh, which always entices us to some evil, but to resist it by the Spirit. We must not be overcome with impatience because of the unthankfulness and contempt of people who abuse Christian liberty. But through the Spirit we must overcome this and all other temptations.

Let no man therefore despair if he often feels the flesh stirring up new battles against the Spirit, or if he cannot find in himself the strength to subdue the flesh and make it obedient to the Spirit. I also desire to have a more valiant and constant heart. Not only do I want a heart that boldly despises the threatenings of tyrants, the heresies, offenses, and tumults which the heretical spirits stir up, but also a heart that might always shake off the troublings and anguish of spirit — even a heart that does not fear the sharpness of death, but receives and embraces it as a most friendly guest. But I find another law in my members, rebelling against the law of my mind.

Therefore, let no man be surprised or dismayed when he feels in himself this battle of the flesh against the Spirit. But let him stir up his heart and comfort himself with Paul's words: "For the flesh lusts against the Spirit, and the Spirit against the flesh; and these are contrary to one another, so that you do not do the things that you would" (Gal. 5:17). By these sentences Paul comforts those who are tempted. In other words, he is saying it is impossible for you to follow the leading of the Spirit in all things without any contrary feeling or hindrance of the flesh. The flesh will resist and hinder in such a way that you cannot do those things that you gladly would. Therefore when a man feels this battle of the flesh, let him not be discouraged with it, but let him resist in the Spirit. In the midst of the battle let him say, "I am a sinner, and I feel sin in me, for I have not yet put off the flesh in which sin dwells as long as the flesh lives. But I will obey the Spirit and not the flesh; that is, I will by faith and hope lay hold upon Christ, and by His word I will raise myself up. And being raised up, I will not fulfill the lust of the flesh."

It is very profitable for believers to know this and to bear it well in mind, for it wonderfully comforts them when they are tempted. When I was a monk I thought that I was utterly cast away if at any time I felt the evil reactions of the flesh, that is, if I felt any evil motion, fleshly lust, wrath, hatred, or envy against any brother. I tried in many outward ways to rid myself of this, but it did not profit me, for the lust of my flesh always returned, so that I could not rest. I was continually disturbed with these accusing thoughts: You have committed this or that sin. You are infected with envy, with impatience, and other such sins. Therefore you have entered into the priesthood in vain, and all your good works are unprofitable.

If then I had rightly understood Paul's words, "For the flesh lusts against the Spirit, and the Spirit against the flesh; and these are contrary to one another, so that you do not do the things that you would," I should not have so miserably tormented myself, but should have thought and said to myself, as I now commonly do, "Martin, you shall not utterly be without sin, for you still have flesh, and you shall feel the battle within, according to Paul's word, 'The flesh resists the Spirit.' Therefore, do not despair, but resist it strongly, and so not fulfill its lust. By doing this you are not under the law."

I remember that my spiritual advisor, Staupitz, was in the habit of saying, "I have vowed to God more than a thousand times that I would become a better man, but I never performed what I vowed. From now on I will make no such vow, for I have now learned by experience that I am not able to perform it. Therefore unless God is favorable and merciful to me for Christ's sake, and grants to me a blessed and a happy hour when I will depart in grace out of this miserable life, I will not be able with all my vows and all my good deeds to stand before Him." This is a true confession for all believers. For the godly do not trust in their own righteousness, but say with David, "Do not enter into judgment with Your servant, for in Your sight shall none that live be justified" (Psa. 143:2), and, "If You, Lord, should mark iniquities, O Lord, who could stand?" (Psa. 130:3).

The godly look to Christ their Reconciler, who gave His life for their sins. They also know that the remnant of sin which is in their flesh is not laid to their charge, but freely pardoned. Yet in the meanwhile they fight in the Spirit against the flesh, so that they should not fulfill its lust. And although they feel the flesh raging and rebelling against the Spirit, and they themselves also may fall sometimes into sin through weakness, yet they are not discouraged, nor do they think that their state and kind of life and the works they do according to their calling displease God, but they raise themselves up by faith.

The faithful therefore receive great comfort by this teaching of Paul's, knowing that they have both the flesh and the Spirit. Yet with the Spirit ruling and the flesh being subdued, righteousness reigns and sin serves. He who does not know this teaching and thinks that believers should be without all fault, and yet sees the opposite in himself, will eventually be swallowed up by the spirit of heaviness and fall into desperation. But whoever knows this teaching well and uses it rightly, to him the things that are evil turn into good. For when the flesh provokes him to sin, it becomes an occasion to be freshly stirred up and forced to seek forgiveness of sins by Christ and to embrace the righteousness of faith. In other words, apart from this inward struggle and battle he would not so greatly appreciate or seek with such great desire the cleansing of the blood and God's righteousness in Christ.

Therefore it is very profitable for us to sometimes feel the wickedness of our nature and corruption of our flesh, that even by this means we may be awakened and stirred up to faith and to call upon Christ. And by this kind of experience a Christian becomes a mighty workman and a wonderful creator, who out of heaviness can make joy, out of terror can create comfort, out of sin can find righteousness, and out of death can enter into life. All of this happens out of the battle with the flesh when in the midst of struggle itself, the flesh is repressed and bridled by being made subject to the Spirit.

Therefore let not those who feel the evil reactions of the flesh despair of their salvation. Though they feel it and all the force of it, yet they do not consent to it. Though the passions of lust, wrath, and other such vices shake them, yet they are not overthrown by them. Though sin violently attacks them, yet they will not let it reign in them. Indeed, the more godly a man is, the more he feels the battle. It is because of this inward battle that those sighs and complaints come from the saints in the Psalms and in all the Holy Scripture. Of this battle the hermits, the monks, and the scholars, and all who seek righteousness and salvation by works, know nothing at all.

But here someone may say that it is dangerous to teach that a man is not condemned if he does not overcome the motions and passions of the flesh that he feels. For when such a doctrine is taught among the common people, it makes them careless, negligent, and slothful. This is what I spoke of a little before, that if we teach faith, then fleshly men neglect and reject works; and if we teach that works are required, then faith and peace of conscience is lost. In this experience no man can be compelled, neither can there be any certain rule set down. But let every man diligently test himself to see what passion of the flesh he is most subject to, and when he finds that, let him not be careless nor flatter himself, but let him watch and wrestle in Spirit against it, so that if he cannot altogether bridle it, yet at least he does not fulfill its lust.

All the saints have had and felt this battle of the flesh against the Spirit, and the same battle we ourselves also feel and know. He who searches his own conscience, if he is not a hypocrite, shall clearly perceive this to be true in himself which Paul says in Galatians 5:17, that "the flesh lusts against the Spirit." All believers therefore do feel and confess that their flesh resists the Spirit, and that these two in themselves are so contrary to each other that, try as they may, they are not able to perform that which they would do. Therefore the flesh hinders us so that we cannot keep the commandments of God, or love our neighbors as ourselves, much less can we love God with all our heart. Therefore it is impossible for us to become righteous by the works of the law. Indeed there is a good will in us, and there must be (for it is the Spirit itself which resists the flesh), which would gladly do good, fulfill the law, love God and his neighbor, and things like these. But the flesh does not obey this good will, but resists it, and yet God does not impute this sin to us, for He is merciful to those that believe, for Christ's sake.

But this does not mean that you should make a light matter of sin because God does not count it against you. It is true that He does not impute it. But to whom, and for what cause? Not to them who are hard-hearted and secure, but to those who repent and lay hold by faith upon Christ the mercy-seat, for whose sake, just as all their sins are forgiven them, even so the remnants of sin which are in them are not imputed to them. They do not view their sin to be less than it is, but openly confess it and call it what it is. They know that it cannot be put away by satisfactions, works, or their own righteousness, but only by the death of Christ. And yet despite the greatness and enormity of their sin, it does not cause them to despair. But they assure themselves that their sin and sins shall not be imputed to them, or laid to their charge, for Christ's sake. [5]

◆

Just as Martin Luther was, you may be troubled in your conscience because of personal sins and wrongdoings. Your conscience is loaded with guilt. Perhaps you have attempted to relieve that guilt by making promises to God, or by making determined resolutions to change your ways, or even by telling someone else about your sins. All these self-made "attempts" have not removed the guilt on your troubled conscience. Why? Because the Bible describes all these attempts as "dead works."

Indeed, the accumulation of guilt on your troubled conscience, as on Luther's, is waiting for you to see and hear the good news of the gospel. The good news is that *God's righteousness* has completely solved your problem. God's way and method of dealing with your troubled conscience is by His righteousness manifested and revealed on the cross of Christ!

When Christ died on the cross and shed His precious blood, God's righteousness was displayed in *how* He solved the problem of sin and guilt. Our sins were laid upon Christ once and for all, and we bear them no more (2 Cor. 5:21). God's righteous character was satisfied with that death (Isa. 53:10-11). It is the blood of Christ, not your own "dead works," that cleanses your conscience. Hebrews 9:14 tells us, "How much more shall the blood of Christ, who through the eternal Spirit offered Himself without spot to God, cleanse your conscience from dead works to serve the living God?"

You may need to repent of your repentance that was based upon dead works, and simply look at God's righteousness manifested on the cross. Only the blood of Jesus Christ can relieve a guilt-ridden conscience. Trust in God's way of solving your problem of sin and guilt through the cross, and you will find Him!

3 John Calvin

• An Arrested Life •

"God by a sudden conversion subdued and brought my mind to a teachable frame."

(1509-1564)

*T*he sovereignty of God was not merely a teaching to John Calvin; it was his experience. Indeed, his life and ministry is characterized by his being "arrested" by God. First, he testifies that he was living a life pursuing the will of his earthly father, in changing from the study of philosophy to law, when "God, by the secret guidance of His providence . . . gave a different direction to my course."[1] Second, Calvin says that while he was steeped in the darkness of Catholic tradition, "God by a sudden conversion subdued and brought my mind to a teachable frame."[2] Third, in relating the account of an overnight stop in Geneva, on his way from Paris to Strasbourg, he says, "William Farel [a zealous French reformer] detained me at Geneva, not so much by counsel and exhortation, as by a dreadful curse, which I felt to be as* *if God had from heaven laid His mighty hand upon me to arrest me."* [3] *Thus, Calvin's life is an example of how God comes into our lives in unexpected ways to get our attention — to arrest us.*

Thank God, He got John Calvin's attention and transformed him into a mighty force in the history of the church for the opening of the truth of God's Word. Calvin was balanced in both the revelation of the Bible and the application of God's truth to a practical church life in Geneva. The work that he did to establish the church life in Geneva was referred to by John Knox, the Scottish reformer, as "the most perfect school of Christ that ever was in the earth since the days of the apostles." [4]

Calvin rarely spoke of himself. His testimony of how he found Christ by a "sudden conversion" has here been pieced together from various sections of his writings:

WHEN I WAS STILL a very little boy, my father had destined me for the study of theology. But afterwards, when he considered that the legal profession made its followers wealthy, this caused him to suddenly change his purpose. So I was withdrawn from the study of philosophy and was enrolled in the study of law. I endeavored faithfully to apply myself to this in obedience to my father's will. But God, by the secret guidance of His providence, later gave a different direction to my course. [5]

I, O Lord,[‡] as I had been educated from a boy, always professed the Christian faith. But at first I had no other reason for my faith than what then prevailed everywhere. Your Word, which should have shone on all Your people like a lamp, was taken away, or at least suppressed. And so that no one would long for greater light, an idea had been instilled into the minds of all that the investigation of that hidden celestial philosophy was better delegated to a few, whom the others might consult as oracles. Thus, it was taught that for common people's minds, the highest knowledge suitable for them was to subdue themselves into obedience to the Church. Also, the principles in which I had been instructed were of a kind that could neither properly train me to the true worship of Your Deity, nor pave the way for me to a sure hope of salvation, nor train me correctly for the duties of the Christian life. Yes, I had learned to worship You alone as my God, but since the true method of worshipping was altogether unknown to me, I stumbled at the very threshold.

I believed, as I had been taught, that I was redeemed by the death of Your Son from being liable to eternal death, but the redemption I knew was one whose benefits could never reach me. I anticipated a future resurrection

---

[‡] Various portions of John Calvin's testimony were written by him in the form of a conversation with the Lord.

but hated to think of it, considering it to be a most dreadful event. And this feeling not only had dominion over me in my private thoughts, but it was derived from the doctrine which was delivered to all the people by their Christian teachers. Yes, they indeed preached of Your mercifulness toward men, but they confined it to those who showed themselves deserving of it.

Moreover, they placed the deserving of it in the righteousness of works, so that only he who reconciled himself to You by works was received into Your favor. And they did not disguise the fact that we are miserable sinners, and that we often fall through weakness of the flesh. Therefore, we needed Your mercy as our common haven of salvation, but the method of obtaining it, they pointed out, was by making satisfaction to You for offenses.

Then, the satisfaction required was, first, after confessing all our sins to a priest, to pray humbly for pardon and absolution; and, secondly, to do good, and by this erase our bad actions from Your remembrance. Lastly, in order to supply what was still lacking, we were to add sacrifices and restitutions to offset our sins. Then, because You were a stern judge and strict avenger of sin, they showed how dreadful Your presence must be. So they directed us to flee first to the saints, that by their intercession You might be rendered entreatable and favorable toward us.

When however I had performed all these things, though I had some periods of quiet, I was still far off from true peace of conscience; for whenever I descended into myself or raised my mind to You, extreme terror seized me — terror which no compensations or satisfactions could cure. And the more closely I examined myself, the sharper were the stings that pricked my conscience, so that the only relief I could find was to delude myself by obliviousness.

Still, as nothing better offered itself, I continued the course that I had begun. But then a very different form of doctrine started up [the Reformation]. It was not one that led us away from the Christian faith, but one that brought it back to its fountainhead, and, so to speak, clearing away the dross, restored it to its original purity. Offended by the novelty, I lent an unwilling ear, and at first, I confess, strenuously and passionately resisted; for (such is the firmness or presumptuous boldness with which it is natural to men to persist in the course that they have undertaken) it was with the greatest difficulty that I confessed I had been in ignorance and error all my life.

One thing in particular made me oppose these new teachers [the reformers], namely, my reverence for the Church. But when I finally opened my ears and allowed myself to be taught, I could see that my fear of detracting from the majesty of the Church was groundless. For they reminded me how great the difference is between separating from the Church, and studying to correct the faults by which the Church herself was contaminated. They spoke nobly of the Church and showed the greatest desire to cultivate unity. They had no problem with the proper meaning of the term *church,* but they showed from the Scriptures and history that it was no new thing for Antichrists to preside in the church in place of pastors. Concerning this they produced many examples, from which it appeared that they aimed at nothing but the building up of the Church, and in that respect were the same as many of Christ's servants whom we ourselves included in the catalog of saints.

These new teachers protested freely against the Roman Pontiff, who was reverenced as "the viceregent of Christ," "the successor of Peter," and "the head of the Church." They pointed out that such titles as those are empty labels of dread, and the eyes of the pious should not be so blinded that they would not dare to look at such titles and sift the reality. It was when the world was plunged in ignorance and sloth, as in a deep sleep, that the Pope had risen to such prominence. Certainly he was neither appointed head of the Church by the Word of God, nor ordained by a legitimate act of the Church, but of his own accord, he was self-elected. Moreover, the tyranny that he let loose against the people of God should not be tolerated if we wished to have the kingdom of Christ among us in safety.

And they had many powerful arguments to confirm all their positions. First, they clearly nullified everything that was then commonly brought forward to establish the primacy of the Pope. When they had taken away all these props, they also, by the Word of God, tumbled him from his lofty height. On the whole, they made it clear and evident to the learned and unlearned that the true order of the Church had been lost and that Christian liberty had fallen — in short, that the kingdom of Christ was prostrated when this primacy was established. Moreover, in order to prick my conscience, they told me that I could not safely disregard these things as if they did not concern me — that You, O Lord, are so far from overlooking any such voluntary error; indeed, even he who is led astray by mere ignorance does not err without punishment. This they proved by the testimony of Your Son: "If the blind lead the blind, both shall fall into the ditch" (Matt. 15:14).

My mind was now prepared for serious attention, and at last I saw, as if light had broken in upon me, in what a style of error I had wallowed, and how much pollution and impurity I had taken in. Being greatly alarmed at the misery I had fallen into, and much more alarmed at what threatened me in view of eternal death, I, as being bound by duty, made it my first business to commit myself to Your way, condemning my past life, not without groans and tears. And now, O Lord, what is left for a wretch like me — not to defend myself, but to earnestly and humbly pray that You would not judge according to what I deserve for my fearful abandonment of Your Word, from which, in Your wondrous goodness, You have at last delivered me. [6]

At first, I was too obstinately devoted to the superstitions of the Papacy to be easily delivered from such a profound abyss of mire. So God by a sudden conversion subdued and brought my mind to a teachable frame, because it had been more hardened in such matters than was normal for one at my young age. Having now received some taste and knowledge of true godliness, I was immediately inflamed with an intense desire to make progress in it. Although I did not altogether drop my other studies, I pursued them with less earnestness.

I was quite surprised to find that before a year had gone by, all who had any desire after purer doctrine were continually coming to me to learn, although I myself was still a mere novice and beginner. Yet my disposition was somewhat unpolished and bashful, causing me to love the shade and retirement. So I began to seek some secluded corner where I might be withdrawn from the public view. But I was unable to accomplish what I desired, because all my retreats became like public schools. In short, my one great object was to live in seclusion without being known. But God so led me about through different turnings and changes that He never permitted me to rest in any place, until, in spite of my natural disposition, He brought me forth to public notice.

Leaving my native country, France, I retired into Germany for the purpose of enjoying in some obscure corner the tranquility which I had always desired, and which had been so long denied me. But lo! while I lay hidden at Basle, and known only to a few people, many faithful and holy persons were burnt alive in France. The report of these burnings reached foreign nations and excited the strongest disapproval among many of the Germans, whose indignation was kindled against the authors of such tyranny. In order to lessen this indignation, certain wicked and lying pamphlets were circulated, stating that none were treated with such cruelty but Anabaptists and the rebellious and disorderly. It was alleged that these, by their perverse ravings and false opinions, were overthrowing not only religion but also all civil order.

I observed the motive behind these allegations: It was not only that the disgrace of shedding so much innocent blood might remain buried under the false charges and slanders which they brought against the holy martyrs after their death, but it was also that afterwards they could proceed to the furthest extent in murdering the poor saints without exciting others' compassion toward them. So it appeared to me that unless I opposed them to the best of my ability, by my silence I would be guilty of cowardice and treachery. This was the consideration that persuaded me to publish my *Institute of the Christian Religion.*

My first object was to prove that these reports were false and slanderous, and thus to vindicate my brethren, whose death was precious in the sight of the Lord. And second, to touch foreign nations, that they might have some compassion and concern for others who might soon be victims of the same cruelties. When it was then published, it was not the extensive and labored work that it now is, but only a small treatise containing a summary of the principal truths of the Christian religion. And it was published with no other purpose than that men might know what was the faith held by those whom I saw basely and wickedly defamed. That my object was not to acquire fame appeared from this — that immediately after, I left Basle; and also that no one there knew I was the author.

Wherever I have gone, I have taken care to conceal that I was the author of that work. And I determined to continue in the same privacy and obscurity, until William Farel detained me at Geneva, not so much by counsel and exhortation, as by a dreadful curse on my retirement and private studies. I felt this to be as if God had from heaven laid His mighty hand upon me to arrest me.

Were I to narrate the various conflicts by which the Lord has exercised me since that time, and the trials by which He has proved me, it would make a long history. But that I may not become tedious to my readers by a waste of words, I will briefly repeat what I have touched upon a little before. That is, in considering the whole course of the life of David, it seemed to me that by his own footsteps he showed me the way, and from this I have experienced great consolation. [7]

I follow David at a great distance and come far short of equaling him. Although in aspiring slowly and with great difficulty to attain to the many virtues in which he excelled, I still feel myself tarnished with the contrary vices. Yet if I have any things in common with him, I have no hesitation in comparing myself with him. In reading the instances of his faith, patience, fervor, zeal, and integrity, it has, as it should, drawn from me countless groans and sighs, because I am so far from approaching them. But nevertheless, it has been a great advantage to me to behold in him, as in a mirror, both the beginning of my calling and the continued course of my function. From this I know with more certainty that whatever that most illustrious king and prophet suffered, it was shown to me by God as an example for imitation.

My condition, no doubt, is much inferior to David's, and it is unnecessary for me to dwell on this. But just as he was taken from the sheepfold and elevated to the rank of supreme authority, so God, having taken me from my originally obscure and humble condition, has counted me worthy of being entrusted with the honorable office of a preacher and minister of the gospel. [8]

———————————◆———————————

John Calvin's testimony of how God came to him in the midst of his various pursuits and "arrested" him matches the Bible's description of how God works out His purpose over our lives. Romans 8:28-31 reveals God's sovereign will over our lives: [28] "And we know that all things work together for good to those who love God, to those who are the called according to His purpose. [29] For whom He foreknew, He also predestined to be conformed to the image of His Son, that He might be the firstborn among many brethren. [30] Moreover whom He predestined, these He also called; whom He called, these He also justified; and whom He justified, these He also glorified. [31] What then shall we say to these things? If God is for us, who can be against us?"

Consider how everything in your life right now is working together for the "good" of God getting your attention. God getting our attention *is* God calling us according to His purpose. And His purpose is to justify us and to glorify us — to conform us to the image of His Son. This is *how* God is for us. God is for you in and through every environment He sends your way. He is for you to find and to love His Son. God loves you. God wants you for Himself. Let His love *arrest* you from your own way. This sudden conversion can happen to you now.

Ephesians 2:3-5 tells us about this sudden conversion — from our being a child of wrath, to our becoming a child of love, mercy, and grace: [3] "We...were by nature children of wrath, just as the others. [4] But God, who is rich in mercy, because of His great love with which He loved us, [5] even when we were dead in trespasses, made us alive together with Christ (by grace you have been saved)."

4 John Bunyan

• Mental Conflict •

"It was not my good feelings
that made my righteousness
better, or my bad feelings
that made my righteousness
worse, for my righteousness
was Jesus Christ Himself."

(1628-1688)

*John Bunyan lived for a period of years in a state of
mental conflict over his sinful condition before God.
Under a constant barrage of accusations from the devil,
he often coped with intense feelings of desperation, guilt,
and fear. But his life was greatly changed one day when
the Holy Spirit quickened to him a verse from the Bible
in which he saw that Jesus Christ Himself was his
righteousness. After this experience Bunyan began to
preach Christ in Bedford, England, and as a result was
imprisoned intermittently from 1660 to 1672. While in
prison he wrote the well-known classic,* Pilgrim's
Progress. *The following is a portion from his autobiography,* Grace Abounding to the Chief of Sinners, *in which he
describes how he found Christ as his righteousness.*

THE TEMPTER BEGAN a new attack by telling me that Christ did pity my case and was sorry for my loss, but that He was helpless to save me from my sins, because they were not the kind for which He had bled and died. My sins were not among those laid to His charge when He died on the cross. By this I concluded that unless He should come down from heaven and die again for my kind of sins, there was no hope for me.

These things may sound ridiculous, but to me they were tormenting thoughts. Every one of them increased my misery. It was not that I felt the power of His cross was weak or somehow that His grace and salvation had already been spent upon others with nothing left for me, but because of His faithfulness to His own threatenings, He could not extend His mercy to me. So all these fears arose from my steadfast belief in the truth of the Word of God while, at the same time, I was misinformed about the nature of my sin.

By these strange and unusual assaults of the tempter, my soul was like a broken vessel driven with the winds and tossed headlong into despair. I was like the man who had his dwelling among the tombs with the dead, who was always crying out and cutting himself with stones (Mark 5:2-5). Oh, the unthinkable imaginations, frights, fears, and terrors that possess a man weighed down by guilt and desperation! Even his desperation will not comfort him. But out of this dreadful experience I did get a deeper realization of the fact that the Scriptures were the Word of God. Oh! I cannot express how clearly I now saw and felt the steadiness of Jesus Christ. I saw Him as the Rock of man's salvation. What He did on the cross could not be undone. What He said could not be unsaid. I saw that the unpardonable sin could drive the soul beyond the help of Christ, and woe unto him who is thus driven, for the word spoken by Christ would shut him out (Mark 3:29). Thus, I was convinced of the faithfulness of His word, but that very word would always sink me in despair in whatever I thought or did.

One day I walked to a neighboring town and sat down upon a bench along the street. I was in deep thought about the terrible state my sin had brought me to. And while I was in this mental state, I lifted my head and thought I saw the sun shining in the heavens in a way that it hated to give me light, and that the very stones in the street and tiles on the houses bent themselves against me. It seemed as though all creation had combined together to banish me out of the world. I was abhorred by creation itself and unfit to dwell among them or be a partaker of their benefits, because I had sinned against the Savior. I saw how much happier every creature was compared to myself. For creation stood fast and kept its station, but I was gone and lost.

Then breaking out in bitterness of my soul I said to myself with a grievous sigh, "How can God comfort such a wretch as I?" I had no sooner said this than there came to me, as an echo answers to a voice: "This sin is not unto death." Suddenly, it was as if I had been raised out of the grave, and I cried out, "Lord, where did You ever find such a wonderful word as this?" For I was filled with admiration at the fitness of the word, at the unexpectedness of the sentence, and the right timing of it. The power, sweetness, light, and glory that came with this word was marvelous to me. Anyone who has gone through this understands what relief came to my soul. The terrible storm was ended, and I now seemed to stand upon the same ground as other sinners and to have as much right to the Word and to prayer as any of them.

A hundred times the tempter sought to break my peace. Oh, the conflicts that I met with now! As I strove to hold to this good word, the enemy made the Scripture about Esau fly in my face like lightning (Heb. 12:16-17). Sometimes I would be up and down twenty times in one hour, yet God helped me and kept my heart upon this word from which I had much sweetness and hope for several days. I felt that He would surely pardon me, for it seemed to me that He was saying, "I loved you *while* you were committing this sin, I loved you *before,* I love you *still,* and I will love you *forever.*"

Then later as I was again in prayer, and trembling under fear that no word of God could help me, that piece of a sentence darted in upon me, "My grace is sufficient"

(2 Cor. 12:9), and I was filled with hope. And yet just about two weeks before, I had been reading this very verse and thought that it was of no help nor comfort to me at all. In fact I threw down the Bible with impatience for I thought at that time it was not large enough to embrace me. But now it seemed as if this verse had arms of grace so wide that it could not only embrace me but many more besides.

I kept on praying that God would show me the complete answer. I knew now that there was a possibility of grace for me, but I could not go further. My first question was answered; there was hope, and God was still merciful. But the second question — was there hope *for me?* — was still unanswered.

One day in a meeting of God's people, I was full of sadness and terror, for my fears were strong upon me again. Suddenly, there broke in upon me this word, "My grace is sufficient for you, My grace is sufficient for you, My grace is sufficient for you." Three times it came. The word was a mighty one for me. At this time my understanding was enlightened, and I felt as though I had seen the Lord Jesus looking down from heaven right through the roof, directing His words right to me. Yet this glory and refreshing did not last long. As usual, the other word concerning Esau came back to me, and there came again that up-and-down experience of now peace and now terror.

Thus I went on for several weeks, sometimes comforted, sometimes tormented. One day I remember wondering what would happen if some verse of terror, such as the one about Esau, should come into my heart at the same moment that there came one of promise and peace. I began to long that this would happen and desired of God that it might be. Well, about two or three days afterward, that is exactly what happened. Both came to me at the same time and worked and struggled strongly in me for a while. But at last, the one about Esau's birthright left and the one about the sufficiency of grace prevailed with peace and joy.

John 6:37 also helped me: "And him who comes to Me I will in no wise cast out." Oh, the comfort that I had through this word, "in no wise." Satan tried hard to pull this promise away from me, saying that Christ did not mean me, that He spoke of sinners who had not done the same thing that I had. But I would answer him, "Satan, there is no exception in these words. 'Him who comes' means any 'him.'" As I look back on this experience, I remember that Satan never once put this further question to me: "But do you come in the right way?" And I think the reason was that he was afraid I would be reminded that to come in the right way was to come as I was, a vile and ungodly sinner, and to cast myself at the feet of mercy. If ever Satan and I strove about anything in the Bible, it was over this word from the Gospel of John.

And, God be praised, I overcame him and got sweetness from the verse.

And now there remained only the end portion of the tempest. The thunder of accusation was gone and only some small drops remained that now and then would fall upon me. But since my former torment was so very sore and deep, I was like those who have been scarred with fire. I thought that every little touch would hurt my tender conscience.

One day as I was passing into the field, suddenly this sentence fell upon my soul: "Your righteousness is in heaven." And I thought that I could see Jesus Christ at God's right hand. Yes, there indeed was my righteousness, so that wherever I was, or whatever I was doing, God could not say about me that I did not have righteousness, for it was standing there before Him. I also saw that it was not my good feelings that made my righteousness better, or my bad feelings that made my righteousness worse, for my righteousness was Jesus Christ Himself, "the same yesterday, and today, and forever" (Heb. 13:8).

Now indeed the chains fell off my legs; I was loosened from my afflictions and irons. My temptations also fled away so that from that time forward those dreadful Scriptures terrified me no more. Now I went home rejoicing because of the grace and love of God, and went to my Bible to look up where the verse was found that said, "Your righteousness is in heaven." But I could not find it. And so my heart began to sink again, until suddenly, there came to my remembrance 1 Corinthians 1:30 — "Christ Jesus, who of God is made unto us wisdom, that is, righteousness and sanctification and redemption." From this, I saw that the other sentence was also true.

I lived here sweetly at peace with God through Christ for a long time. There was nothing but Christ before my eyes. Now I was not thinking of Him only in relation to His blood, His burial, or His resurrection, but I was thinking of Christ Himself, and that He sat there on the right hand of God in heaven.

I gloried to see His exaltation and the wonders of His benefits which He so readily bestowed. I saw that all those graces of God that belonged to me, but which I displayed so little of, were like those few coins that rich men used to carry in their purses while their gold was in their trunks at home. I saw that my gold was in my trunk at Home — in Christ, my Lord and Savior. Now Christ was all — all my righteousness, all my sanctification, and all my redemption.

The Lord also led me into the mystery of union with the Son of God, and I saw that I was joined to Him, that I was flesh of His flesh and bone of His bone (Eph. 5:30). And if He and I were one, then His righteousness was mine, His merits mine, His victory also mine. Now I could see myself in heaven and on earth at the same time;

in heaven by my Christ, my Head, my Righteousness and my Life; and on earth by my own body.

I saw that we fulfilled the law by Him, died by Him, rose from the dead by Him, got the victory over sin, death, the devil, and hell by Him. When He died, we died, and so it was also with His resurrection: "After two days He will revive us; on the third day He will raise us up, and we shall live in His sight" (Hosea 6:2). This is now fulfilled as the Son of Man sits down on "the right hand of the Majesty in the heavens," as it says, He "has raised us up together, and made us sit together in heavenly places in Christ Jesus" (Eph. 2:6). Oh, praise the Lord for all the Scriptures! [1]

Like John Bunyan, you may find yourself in a state of severe mental conflict over your sinful condition before God. What you need to see is what Bunyan saw in 1 Corinthians 1:30: "But of Him you are in Christ Jesus, who became for us wisdom from God — that is, righteousness and sanctification and redemption." Consider now that God has made Christ *your* righteousness. Do not seek to establish your own righteousness and to justify yourself before God, but accept Christ as the righteousness of God (Rom. 10:3-4).

Isaiah 64:6 declares, "But we are all like an unclean thing, and all our righteousnesses are like filthy rags."

Thus, what you need to do is simply follow the Word of God in Romans, which says, [9] "If you *confess* with your mouth the Lord Jesus and *believe* in your heart that God has raised Him from the dead, *you will be saved.* [10] For with the heart one believes to righteousness, and with the mouth confession is made to salvation.... [13] For whoever calls upon the name of the LORD shall be saved" (10:9-10,13). By receiving Christ now and confessing His name, you will know that *your* righteousness is Jesus Christ Himself.

5 Madame Guyon

• A Searching Heart •

"Madame...you seek
without what you have
within...seek God in
your heart, and you
will find Him there."

(1648-1717)

The influence of Madame Guyon's inner life experiences of the Lord has filtered down to many of the most spiritually-minded saints in the history of the church —John Wesley, Hermann Francke, Andrew Murray, Jessie Penn-Lewis, Watchman Nee, and countless others.

The revelation of Christ that transformed her entire life was the simple discovery that Christ was in her. This was similar to the apostle Paul's revelation in Galatians 1:16. Prior to that time she had passed through a long journey of searching after God. As a young girl she had sought for God under her Roman Catholic environment and understanding. She kept times of private prayer, visited the poor, read devotional books, subjected herself to bodily austerities, made vows, and even made a resolution to enter a convent to become a nun.

While she was searching for God, Madame passed through periods in which He allowed her to see the depths of her corruption. During one of these times, she was living in Paris and, under God's dealing, was left to herself. She became vain in her deportment, read romance novels, became proud of her beauty, spent a good deal of her time in front of the mirror, appeared in public to be noticed, and received several marriage proposals.

About this time her father arranged a marriage for her. She did not meet her husband-to-be until three days before their wedding. She soon saw that this marriage was to be "a house of mourning" for her in which all her earthly hopes were "blasted." Many trials, sorrows, and sufferings followed in her domestic environment. Her unpleasant mother-in-law, who lived with them, constantly influenced Madame's husband against her. Madame felt like a slave in her own household.

In the midst of these troubles, she passed through cycles of searching after God, in which she made new resolutions to change and then found herself breaking those resolutions. While experiencing this state of failure and defeat, she came in contact with three people who were used by God to direct her to Christ. One was a truly pious lady who was able to discern and point out that Madame was seeking the Lord "by a system of works without faith." Through her, Madame realized that she was trying to gain by efforts what could only be gained by ceasing from efforts. The second person who deeply touched her was her missionary cousin. When he visited her, he expressed a relationship with Christ that caused her to long for what he had. And finally, the Lord brought a devout man of the order of St. Francis to visit her father. The man had spent five years in solitude, and was afterward divinely led to her father's house. It was to this godly man that Madame opened up her dissatisfaction with her spiritual condition.

From the influence of these three persons, Madame Guyon was led to discover the riches of an indwelling Christ. Here in her own words she tells the story:

I NOW APPLIED MYSELF to my duties, never failing to practice prayer twice a day. I watched over myself continually to control my temper. I went to visit the poor in their houses, assisting them in their distresses. I did (according to my understanding) all the good I knew.

You,[‡] O my God, increased both my love and my patience in proportion to my sufferings. I did not regret my mother favoring my brother above me. I also had for some time severe fits of fever. This illness was very

---

[‡] Madame Guyon wrote her autobiography in the form of a conversation with the Lord.

useful to me. It threw a great light for me on the worthlessness of the things of the world. It detached me much from myself. I even felt that Your love, O my God, was strengthening itself in my heart, with the desire to please You and to be faithful to You in my condition. Yet I did not serve You with that fervor which You gave to me soon after. For I would still have been glad to reconcile Your love with the love of myself and of the creature. Unhappily I always found some who loved me, and whom I could not keep from wishing to please. It was not that I loved them, but it was for the love that I had for myself.

You permitted, O my God, a lady, an exile, to come to my father's house. He offered her an apartment which she accepted, and she stayed a long time. She was one of true piety and inward devotion. She had a great esteem for me because I desired to love God. She remarked that I had the virtues of an active and bustling life, but that I had not yet attained the simplicity of prayer which she experienced. Sometimes she dropped a word to me on that subject. But as my time had not yet come, I did not understand her. Her example instructed me more than her words. I observed on her countenance something which showed a great enjoyment of the presence of God. I endeavored, through studied reflection and thoughts, to possess a continual presence of God. I gave myself much trouble, but made no advance. I wanted to have, by my own efforts, what I could not acquire except by ceasing from all efforts.

My father's nephew had returned from Cochin China to take back some priests from Europe. I was delighted to see him, for I remembered the good his former visit had brought me. The lady who had been exiled rejoiced as much as I did, for they understood each other immediately and talked the same spiritual language. The virtue of this excellent relative charmed me. I admired his continual prayer though I was not able to comprehend it.

I attempted to meditate continually, to think unceasingly of You, O my God, and to utter prayers and short praises. But I could not acquire, by all my toil, what You Yourself at length gave me, and which is experienced only in simplicity. My cousin did all he could to attach me more strongly to You, O my God. He had great affection for me. The purity he observed in me from the corruptions of the age, the abhorrence of sin at a time of life when others are beginning to relish the pleasures of it (I was not yet eighteen), gave him a great tenderness for me. I complained to him of my faults in a transparent way. These I saw clearly. But because the difficulty I found in correcting them made me lose courage, he cheered and exhorted me to persevere in my good endeavors. He would gladly have introduced me into a more simple manner of prayer, but I was not yet ready for it. I believe his prayers were more effectual than his words.

No sooner was he gone out of my father's house, than You, O my Divine Love, had compassion on me. The desire I had to please You, the tears I shed, my great labor and pains, and the little fruit I reaped from it, moved You with compassion. This was the state of my soul when Your goodness, surpassing all my vileness and unfaithfulness, and abounding in proportion to my wretchedness, granted me in a moment what all my own efforts could never earn. Seeing me rowing with so much toil, helpless, You sent, O my Divine Savior, the favorable breath of Your divine operations to carry me full sail over this sea of affliction.

I had often spoken to my confessor about the great anxiety it gave me to find I could not meditate, nor exert my imagination in order to pray. Subjects of prayer that were too extensive were useless to me. Those that were short and pointed suited me better.

Finally, God permitted a very religious person, of the order of St. Francis, to pass by my father's dwelling. He had intended going another way that was a shorter route, but a secret power changed his plans. He saw there was something for him to do, and imagined that God had called him for the conversion of a man of some distinction. Yet his labors proved fruitless. It was the conquest of my soul that was designed. As soon as he arrived he went to see my father, who was very glad of it, but was at the same time very ill and near death.

At this time I was about to give birth to my second son. For some time my father's illness had been concealed from me, but an indiscreet person abruptly told me. Instantly I arose, weak as I was, and went to see him. My father was recovered, but not entirely, yet enough to give me new marks of his affection. I told him of my strong desire to love You, O my God, and my great sorrow at not being able to do it fully. He thought he could not give me a more solid indication of his love than by arranging a visit for me with this worthy man. He told me what he knew of him and urged me to go and see him.

At first I was unwilling to do it, being intent on observing the rules of the strictest modesty. However, my father's repeated requests had with me the weight of a positive command. I thought no harm could come to me from doing something only to obey him. I took one of my relatives with me. At first this good man seemed a little confused, because he was reserved toward women. Having recently come out of five years' solitude, he was surprised that I was the first to talk with him. He did not speak a word for some time. I did not know what to attribute his silence to. I did not hesitate to speak to him and to tell him in a few words about my difficulties concerning prayer. He answered me at once, "It is, Madame, because you seek without what you have within. Accustom yourself to seek God in your heart, and you will find Him there." [1]

Having said these words, the Franciscan left me. They were to me like the stroke of a dart which pierced my heart through and through. I felt at this instant deeply wounded with the love of God — a wound so delightful that I desired never to be healed of it. These words brought into my heart what I had been seeking so many years; or rather they made me discover what was there, which I did not enjoy for lack of knowing it. Oh, my Lord! You were in my heart, and You asked from me only a simple turning inward to make me feel Your presence. Oh, infinite Goodness, You were so near, and I ran here and there seeking You, and yet I did not find You. My life was miserable, yet all the while my happiness was within me. I was poor in the midst of riches and ready to perish with hunger near a table plentifully spread and a continual feast. O Beauty, ancient and new! Why have I known You so late? Alas, I was seeking You where You were not, and I did not seek You where You were! It was for lack of understanding those words of Your Gospel: *"The kingdom of God comes not with observation, neither shall they say, Lo, here! or lo, there! for behold, the kingdom of God is within you."* This I now experienced, since You did become my King, and my heart Your kingdom, where You do reign a Sovereign and do all Your will.

I told this good man that I did not know what he had done to me, that my heart was quite changed, that God was there, and I no longer had any trouble finding Him. For from that moment He had given me an experience of His presence in my soul — not merely as an object intellectually perceived, but as a thing really possessed after the sweetest manner. I experienced those words in the Song of Songs: *"Your name is as precious ointment poured forth; therefore do the virgins love You."* For I felt in my soul an unction, which healed in a moment all my wounds. I did not sleep at all that night, because Your love, O my God, flowed in me like delightful oil, and burned as a fire to destroy all that was left of self in an instant. I was all of a sudden so changed that I was no longer recognizable either to myself or to others. I no longer found those troublesome faults, or that reluctance to duty, which formerly characterized me. They all disappeared, as being consumed like chaff in a great fire.

I now desired that the one who was instrumental in all of this would become my Director. This good father, however, could not readily resolve to undertake my direction, though he saw so surprising a change effected by the hand of God. Several reasons led him to excuse himself: first, my person, then my youth, for I was only twenty years of age; and lastly, a promise he had made to God, from a distrust of himself, never to take upon himself the direction of any female, unless God, by some particular providence, should charge him with it. Upon my earnest and repeated request to him to become my

Director, he said he would pray to God about it, and he charged me to do so too. As he was in prayer, it was said to him, "Do not fear to take charge of her. She is My spouse." This, when I heard it, affected me greatly. "What!" (said I to myself) "a frightful monster of iniquity, who has done so much to offend my God, in abusing His favors and repaying them with ingratitude — and now, to be declared His spouse!" After this he consented to my request.

Nothing was now more easy for me than to pray. Hours passed away like moments, while I could hardly do anything else but pray. The fervency of my love allowed me no intermission. It was a prayer of rejoicing and of possession, in which the taste of God was so great, so pure, unblended, and uninterrupted that it attracted and absorbed the powers of the soul into a profound recollection. It was a state of confiding and affectionate rest in God, existing without intellectual effort. For I now had no sight but of Jesus Christ alone. All else was excluded, in order to love with greater purity and energy, without any motives or reasons for loving which were of a selfish nature. [2]

That sovereign of the powers of the soul — the will — swallowed up the two others, the memory and understanding, into itself and concentrated them in LOVE. They still subsisted, but their operations were in a manner imperceptible and passive. They were no longer stopped or retarded by the multiplicity, but collected and united in one; just as the rising of the sun does not extinguish the stars, but overpowers and absorbs them in the luster of its incomparable glory. [3]

The following remarks by Thomas C. Upham, Madame Guyon's primary biographer, are fitting here:

Such are the expressions in which she speaks of the remarkable change which thus passed upon her spirit — an event which opened new views, originated new feelings, established new relations, and gave new strength. Too important in itself and its relations to be forgotten under any circumstances, we find her often reflecting on it with those confiding, affectionate, and grateful sentiments, which it was naturally calculated to inspire. One of her poems, which Cowper has translated, expresses well the feelings which we may suppose to have existed in her at this time:

Love and Gratitude

All are indebted much to Thee,
But I far more than all
From many a deadly snare set free,
And raised from many a fall.
Overwhelm me from above,
Daily with Thy boundless love.

What bonds of gratitude I feel,
No language can declare;
Beneath the oppressive weight I reel,
'Tis more than I can bear;
When shall I that blessing prove,
To return Thee love for love?

Spirit of Charity! Dispense
Thy grace to every heart;
Expel all other spirits thence;
Drive self from every part.
Charity divine! Draw nigh;
Break the chains in which we lie.

All selfish souls, whate'er they feign,
Have still a slavish lot;
They boast of liberty in vain,
Of love, and feel it not.
He, whose bosom glows with Thee,
He, and he alone, is free.

O blessedness all bliss above,
When Thy pure fires prevail!
LOVE* *only teaches what is love;*
All other lessons fail;
We learn its name, but not its powers,
Experience only makes it ours. [4]

---

* God is *Love,* 1 Jn. 4:8

♦

Madame Guyon's long search to find an indwelling Christ may be similar to your own experience. Perhaps you have sought Him in the wrong places. It is possible to practice religious traditions and rituals and yet not find Christ. Like Madame, you can even be doing the right "spiritual" things and still miss Him.

The woman at the well in John 4 also had a concept of finding God in outward places. In verse 20 she said to Jesus, "Our fathers worshipped on this mountain, and you Jews say that in Jerusalem is the place where one ought to worship." Her seeking was fixed on outward things. But Jesus turned her away from outward religious things to find Him in her spirit. In verses 21-24 He says, [21] "Woman, believe Me, the hour is coming when you will neither on this mountain, nor in Jerusalem, worship the Father.... [23] But the hour is coming, and now is, when the true worshippers will worship the Father in spirit and truth; for the Father is seeking such to worship Him. [24] God is Spirit, and those who worship Him must worship in spirit and truth."

Madame Guyon had been seeking *without* what she had *within.* In the same way, God's work over us is on the inside. That is the meaning of regeneration — Another Life enters into your spirit. Jesus Christ comes into you to impart His life into your deepest part, your human spirit. He becomes an inner source, an inner supply, an inner fountain. He Himself becomes your life (Col. 3:4).

It is "not by works of righteousness which we have done, but according to His mercy He saved us, through the washing of regeneration and renewing of the Holy Spirit" (Titus 3:5). The washing of regeneration and renewing of the Holy Spirit speak of the inner work of God that is done in us and to us.

You need not prolong your frustration and your failure in seeking to find Him. He is in your mouth and in your heart, and now if you "confess with your mouth the Lord Jesus and believe in your heart that God has raised Him from the dead, you will be saved" (Rom. 10:8-9). You will find Him within by His name (John 20:31). The Christ without will become to you the Christ within.

6 John Wesley

• A Defeated Life •

"About a quarter before nine…I felt my heart strangely warmed. I felt I did trust in Christ, Christ alone for salvation."

(1703-1791)

The fifteenth child in his family, John Wesley was raised in a religiously strict home. He was educated at Oxford and ordained as a deacon in the Anglican Church. In 1735 he left England as a missionary to America to preach to the Indians. However, the complete failure of his missionary efforts, coupled with his inability to overcome sin in his own personal life, caused Wesley to evaluate his actual state before God. He was a defeated man. It was then that he began to realize that he had never had a personal encounter with Christ.

After returning to England, he attended a meeting on May 24, 1738, in which Luther's preface to the Epistle to the Romans *was being read. During the reading his heart was "strangely warmed," and that night Wesley found Christ. From that point on, his outdoor preaching throughout Great Britain brought thousands to Christ. The following is an excerpt from his journals, dated May 24th and 25th, 1738, describing his experience of finding Christ:*

I THINK IT IS BEST to give a larger context of what happened to me on Wednesday the 24th so that it will be better understood. Let him who cannot receive it ask of the Father of lights that He would give more light to him and me.

I believe until I was about ten years old I had not sinned away that "washing of the Holy Spirit" which was given me in baptism; having been strictly educated and carefully taught that I could only be saved "by universal obedience, by keeping all the commandments of God." I was diligently instructed as to the meaning of these commandments. And those instructions, so far as they related to outward duties and sins, I gladly received and often thought about. But all that was said to me of inward obedience or holiness I neither understood nor remembered. So I was indeed as ignorant of the true meaning of the law as I was of the gospel of Christ.

I spent the next six or seven years at school. There, outward restraints being removed, I was much more negligent than before, even of outward duties. And I was almost continually guilty of outward sins, which I knew to be such, though they were not scandalous in the eyes of the world. However, I still read the Scriptures and said my prayers morning and evening. And what I now hoped to be saved by was (1) not being so bad as other people; (2) having still a kindness for religion; and (3) reading the Bible, going to church, and saying my prayers.

Being removed to the University for five years, I still said my prayers both in public and in private, and read, with the Scriptures, several other books of religion, especially comments on the New Testament. Yet all this time I did not have so much as a notion of inward holiness. In fact, I went on habitually in some or other known sin, and for the most part very contentedly. However, I did have some interruption and small struggles, especially before and after the Holy Communion, which I was required to receive three times a year. I cannot tell what I then hoped to be saved by, since I was continually sinning against the little light I had, unless it was by those passing fits of what many religious teachers taught me to call repentance.

When I was about twenty-two, my father pressed me to enter into holy orders. At the same time, the providence of God directing me to Kempis's *Christian Pattern,* I began to see that true religion was seated in the heart and that God's law extended to all our thoughts as well as words and actions. I was, however, very angry at Kempis for being too strict. Yet I frequently was very comforted while reading him, though I was an utter stranger to his writings before that time. Also, by spending time with a religious friend, which I never had until now, I began to alter the whole form of my behavior and to earnestly try to start a new life. I set apart an hour or two a day for religious retirement. I took holy communion every week. I watched against all sin, whether in word or deed. I began to aim at, and pray for, inward holiness. So that now, "doing so much and living so good a life," I did not doubt that I was a good Christian.

In 1730 I began visiting the prisons, assisting the poor and sick in town, and doing what other good I could, by my presence or my little fortune, to the bodies and souls of all men. For this purpose I reduced all the excesses in my life, and many things that are considered the necessities of life. Yet when, after continuing some years in this way, I felt myself to be near death, I could not find that all these ascetic practices gave me any comfort or any assurance of acceptance with God. I was then very surprised at this, not realizing I had been all this time building on the sand, or considering that "other foundation can no man lay than that which is laid" by God, "even Jesus Christ."

Soon after, a spiritually minded man convinced me, even more than I had been convinced, that outward works are nothing by themselves. And in several conversations he instructed me in how to pursue inward holiness, or a union of the soul with God. But even concerning his instructions (though I then received them as the words of God) I now realize (1) he spoke so loosely against trusting in outward works that he discouraged me from doing them at all; (2) he recommended *mental prayer* and similar exercises as the most effectual means of purifying the soul and uniting it with God. Now these were, in reality, as much my own works as visiting the sick or clothing the naked. Pursuing this kind of union with God was as much my own righteousness as any I had previously pursued under another name.

In this refined way of trusting to my own works and my own righteousness (so zealously taught by the Mystic writers), I dragged on heavily, finding no comfort or help in this way of pursuing God, until the time of my leaving England. On shipboard, however, I was again active in outward works, where it pleased God out of His free mercy to give me twenty-six of the Moravian brethren for companions, who endeavored to show me "a more excellent way." But I did not understand it at first. I was too learned and too wise in myself, so it seemed foolish to me. And I continued preaching while following after and trusting in that righteousness by which no flesh can be justified.

All the time I was in Savannah, Georgia, I was beating the air. Being ignorant of the righteousness of Christ, which, by a living faith in Him, brings salvation "to every one who believes," I sought to establish my own righteousness, and so labored in the fire all my days. I was now properly "under the law." I knew that the law of God was spiritual, and I consented to it that it was good. Yes, I delighted in it, according to the inner man. Yet I was fleshly, sold under sin. Every day I was constrained to cry out, "What I do, I know not: for what I would, I do not; but what I hate, that I do. To will is indeed present with me; but how to perform that which is good, I find not. For the good which I would, I do not; but the evil which I would not, that I do. I find a law, that when I would do good, evil is present with me: even the law in my members, warring against the law of my mind, and still bringing me into captivity to the law of sin" (cf. Rom. 7:13-23).

In this vile, miserable state of bondage to sin, I was indeed fighting continually, but not conquering. Before, I had willingly served sin, but now it was unwillingly, but I still served it. I fell, and rose, and fell again. Sometimes I was overcome and in heaviness; sometimes I overcame and was in joy. Just as in my former state I had some foretastes of the terrors of the law, so now in this experience, I had samples of the comforts of the gospel. During this whole struggle between nature and grace, which had now continued for more than ten years, I had many remarkable returns to prayer, especially when I was in trouble. I had many comforts, which are indeed nothing but short anticipations of the life of faith. But I was still "under the law," not "under grace" (the state most Christians are content to live and die in); for I was only striving with sin, not freed from it. Neither did I have the witness of the Spirit with my spirit, and indeed could not, for I "sought it not by faith, but as it were by the works of the law."

On my return to England in January 1738, I was in imminent danger of death, and became very uneasy because of it. I was strongly convinced that the cause of that uneasiness was unbelief, and that the gaining of a true and living faith was the "one thing needful" for me. But I still did not fix this faith on its right object. I thought it meant only faith in God, not faith in or through Christ. Again, I did not know that I was totally void of this faith, but only thought I did not have enough of it. So when Peter Böhler, whom God prepared for me as soon as I came to London, spoke to me of true faith in Christ (which is but one) and that it had those two fruits inseparably accompanying it, that is, "dominion over sin and constant peace from a sense of forgiveness," I was quite amazed and looked upon it as a new gospel. If this was so, it was clear I did not have faith. But I was not willing to be convinced of this. Therefore, I disputed with all my might, and labored to prove that faith might be where these were not. All the Scriptures related to this matter I had long since been taught to interpret away, and to call all who spoke otherwise "Presbyterians." Besides,

I clearly saw that no one could, in the nature of things, have such a sense of forgiveness and not *feel* it. But I did not feel it. If, then, there was no faith without a sense of forgiveness, all my claims to having faith dropped at once.

When I met Peter Böhler again, he consented to place the dispute on the issue which I desired, namely, Scripture and experience. I first consulted the Scripture. But when I set aside man's interpretation and simply considered the words of God, comparing them together, endeavoring to illustrate the obscure by the plainer passages, I found they were all against me. Then I was forced to retreat to my last hold — that experience would never agree with the *literal interpretation* of those Scriptures. Neither could I therefore allow it to be true, until I found some living witnesses of it. Peter replied that he could show me such at any time, if I desired it, even the next day.

And accordingly, the next day he came again with three others, all of whom testified of their own personal experience, that a true living faith in Christ is inseparable from a sense of pardon for all past sins, and freedom from all present sins. They testified with one mouth that this faith was the gift, the free gift of God, and that He would surely bestow it upon every soul who earnestly and perseveringly sought it. I was now thoroughly convinced, and by the grace of God I resolved to seek it to the end (1) by absolutely renouncing all dependence, in whole or in part, upon *my own* works or righteousness, on which I had really grounded my hope of salvation, though I did not know it, from my youth up; (2) by adding to the constant use of all the other means of grace, continual prayer for this very thing — justifying, saving faith, a full reliance on the blood of Christ shed for *me;* a trust in Him as *my* Christ, as *my* sole justification, sanctification, and redemption.

I continued thus to seek it (though with strange indifference, dullness, and coldness, and unusually frequent relapses into sin) until Wednesday, May 24th. I think it was about five this morning that I opened my Testament on these words, "There are given unto us exceeding great and precious promises, even that you should be partakers of the divine nature" (2 Pet. 1:4). Just as I went out, I opened it again on these words, "You are not far from the kingdom of God." In the afternoon I was asked to go to St. Paul's. The anthem was, "Out of the depths I have called unto You, O Lord; Lord, hear my voice! O let Your ears consider well the voice of my complaint. If You, Lord, should mark iniquities, O Lord, who could stand? But there is mercy with You, that You may be feared. O Israel, trust in the Lord; for with the Lord there is mercy, and with Him is abundant redemption. And He shall redeem Israel from all his sins."

In the evening I went very unwillingly to a society on Aldersgate Street, where someone was reading Luther's preface to the *Epistle to the Romans.* About a quarter before nine, while he was describing the change which God works in the heart through faith in Christ, I felt my heart strangely warmed. I felt I did trust in Christ, Christ alone for salvation; and an assurance was given me that He had taken away *my* sins, even *mine,* and saved *me* from the law of sin and death.

I began to pray with all my might for those who in a more particular way had despitefully used me and persecuted me. I then testified openly to all who were there what I now felt in my heart. But it was not long before the enemy suggested, "This cannot be faith, for where is your joy?" Then I was taught that peace and victory over sin are wholly bound up with faith in the Captain of our salvation. As to the rapturous joy that usually accompanies the beginning of salvation, especially in those who have mourned deeply, God sometimes gives and sometimes withholds these feelings, according to the counsels of His own will.

After my return home, I was greatly bothered by temptations, but cried out, and they fled away. They returned again and again. As often as the temptations came, I lifted up my eyes, and He "sent me help from His holy place." It was in this experience that I found what the difference was between now and my former state. Before, I was striving, yes, even fighting with all my might under the law, as well as under grace, and I was sometimes, if not often, conquered. But now, I was always conqueror. [1]

---◆---

Perhaps you have a personal history similar to John Wesley's — outwardly you have lived a religious life, but inwardly you have discovered that you don't have the ability to overcome sin. You are a defeated person in light of what you know you should be. What you need to hear is what Wesley heard the night he found Christ. He was listening to Luther's words that describe the change that God works in the heart through faith in Christ. The following is the part of Luther's preface referred to by Wesley:

> Faith is a divine work in us, which transforms us, gives us a new birth out of God (John 1:13), slays the old Adam, makes us altogether different men in heart, affection, mind, and all powers, and brings with it the Holy Spirit. Oh, it is a living, energetic, active, mighty thing, this faith! It cannot but do good unceasingly. There is no question asked whether good works are to be done, but before the question is asked the works have been done, and there is a continuous doing of them. But any person not doing such works is without faith. He is groping in the dark, looking for faith and good works, and knows neither what faith is nor what good works are, although he indulges in a lot of twaddle and nonsense concerning faith and good works.
>
> Faith is a living, daring confidence in the grace of God, of such assurance that it would risk a thousand

deaths. This confidence and knowledge of divine grace makes a person happy, bold, and full of gladness in his relation to God and all creatures. The Holy Spirit is doing this in the believer. Hence it is that a person, without constraint, becomes willing and enthusiastic to do good to everybody, to serve everybody, to suffer all manner of afflictions, from love of God and to the praise of Him who has extended such grace to him. Accordingly, it is impossible to separate works from faith, just as impossible as it is to separate the power to burn and shine from fire. Accordingly, beware of your own false thoughts and of idle talkers, who pretend great wisdom for discerning faith and good works and yet are the greatest fools. Pray God that He may create faith in you; otherwise you will be without faith forever and aye, no matter what you may plan and do. [2]

Your defeated life can turn into victory now by trusting in Christ *alone* for your salvation. Acts 4:12 says, "Neither is there salvation in any other: for there is *none* other name under heaven given among men, whereby we must be saved." Turn from your own works and striving. Give up your self-effort and turn this hour to Christ alone for the assurance of your salvation. Wesley could recall that it was "about a quarter before nine." As you are opening to Christ now, mark the time of your "new birth."

7 Jonathan Edwards

• Miserable Seeking •

"The first instance of that sort of inward, sweet delight in God and divine things… was a new sense, quite different from anything I had ever experienced."

(1703-1758)

*J*onathan Edwards is known in the history of the church for the major part he played in the first Great Awakening in America. He succeeded his well-known grandfather, Solomon Stoddard, a Puritan minister of Northhampton, Massachusetts. Stoddard was a man of God whose life was characterized by a deep desire to win the lost to Christ, a love for the Word, and a burden to see the church raised out of its lukewarm state. It was under this kind of atmosphere and influence that Jonathan Edwards was brought up.

In his early years, Jonathan Edwards was the subject of much prayer by his parents. He also had several occasions where he received "strong religious impressions," but they were only of a temporary nature. His own testimony reveals that although he was at times *stirred up to pray, it soon wore off and he returned to his former ways. He admits to going through a period of "great and violent inward struggles, till after many conflicts with wicked inclinations, repeated resolutions and self-reflection," he made seeking salvation the main business of his life. But he describes his seeking as a "miserable seeking."*

The contrast between this miserable state and what Edwards experienced when the Lord came into him is seen in his repeated use of the words "sweet" and "sweetness." If we could pick the one word that describes his inner experience of the Lord, it would be the word "sweet."

*The following are a few samples of the expressions he used to describe the sweetness he found in Christ: "**Sweet** delight in God...an inward, **sweet** sense...**sweetly** conversing with Christ...so **sweet** a sense of the glorious majesty and grace of God...an awful **sweetness**...the **sweet** glory of God...many **sweet** hours...those **sweet** and powerful words...a **sweet** and refreshing season walking alone in the fields."*

Edwards describes in his own words how he passed out of a miserable state into a state of sweetness at the time he found the Lord:

I HAD A VARIETY OF RELIGIOUS concerns about my soul from my childhood. But I had two remarkable seasons of awakening before I met with that change that brought me to those new dispositions and that new sense of things that I have had since. The first time was when I was a boy, some years before I went to college, at a time of remarkable awakening in my father's congregation. I was then very much affected for many months and concerned about the things of religion and my soul's salvation. And I was also abundant in religious duties. I used to pray five times a day in secret and to spend much time in religious conversation with other boys and meet with them to pray together.

I experienced a certain kind of delight in religion. My mind was very engaged in it and I had much self-righteous pleasure from it. It was my delight to abound in religious duties. I, with some of my schoolmates, joined together and built a booth in a swamp in a very hidden spot, for a place of prayer. And besides, I had particular secret places of my own in the woods, where I used to go by myself, and was from time to time much affected. My affections seemed to be lively and easily moved, and I seemed to be in my element when I engaged in religious duties. And I believe that many are deceived with such affections and delights as I then had in religion, and that they mistake it for grace.

But over time my convictions and affections wore off. I entirely lost all those affections and delights and abandoned my habit of secret prayer. I returned like a dog to his vomit and went on in the ways of sin. Indeed, I was at times very uneasy, especially toward the latter part of my time at college. At this time it pleased God to seize me with a pleurisy, in which He brought me near to the grave and shook me over the pit of hell. And yet it was not long after my recovery before I fell again into my old ways of sin.

But God would not permit me to go on with any quietness. I had great and violent inward struggles. But after many conflicts with wicked inclinations, repeated resolutions, and bonds that I laid myself under by a kind of vow to God, I was brought wholly to break off all former wicked ways and all ways of known outward sin. I applied myself to seek salvation and practice many religious duties, but without that kind of affection and delight which I had formerly experienced. My concern for salvation now came more because of inward struggles and conflicts and self-reflections.

I made seeking my salvation the main business of my life. Yet, it seems to me I sought it in a miserable way, which has since made me sometimes question whether my seeking ever issued in that which was saving. Now I doubt whether such miserable seeking ever succeeded. I was indeed brought to seek salvation in a manner that I never had before. I felt drawn to part with all things in the world for an interest in Christ. My concern to be saved continued and prevailed with many cogitations and inward struggles, yet it never seemed to be proper to say that it was motivated by terror.

From my childhood up, my mind had been full of objections against the doctrine of God's sovereignty — in choosing whom He would to eternal life, and rejecting whom He pleased, leaving them eternally to perish and be everlastingly tormented in hell. It appeared like a horrible doctrine to me. But I remember the time very well when I seemed to be convinced and fully satisfied as to this sovereignty of God and His justice in eternally dealing with men according to His sovereign pleasure. But I never could give an account of how, or by what means, I was convinced. I could not imagine that there was any extraordinary influence of God's Spirit in it. I only know that now I saw further, and my reason apprehended the justice and reasonableness of God's sovereignty. My mind rested in it, and this put an end to all those complaints and objections. There has been a wonderful change in my mind with respect to the doctrine of God's sovereignty from that day to this. So I scarcely ever found a rising objection against it in its most absolute sense — in God showing mercy to whom He will show mercy and hardening whom He will.

God's absolute sovereignty and justice with respect to salvation and damnation is what my mind seems to rest assured of, as much as of anything that I see with my eyes. At least it is so at times. But I have often, since that first conviction, had quite another kind of sense of God's sovereignty. I have had not only a conviction, but a *delightful* conviction. The doctrine has very often appeared exceedingly pleasant, bright, and sweet. Absolute sovereignty is what I love to ascribe to God. But my first conviction was not so.

The first instance I remember of that sort of inward, sweet delight in God and divine things, which I have lived much in since, was on reading those words in 1 Timothy 1:17, "Now unto the King eternal, immortal, invisible, the only wise God, be honor and glory forever and ever. Amen." As I read the words, there came into my soul and was, as it were, diffused through it, a sense of the glory of the Divine Being. It was a new sense, quite different from anything I had ever experienced. Never any words of Scripture seemed to me as these words did. I thought to myself, how excellent a Being that was and how happy I should be if I might enjoy that God, be rapt up to Him in heaven, and be swallowed up in Him forever! I kept saying and singing to myself these words of Scripture. I prayed to God that I might enjoy Him, praying in a manner quite different from what I used to do, with a new sort of affection. But it never came into my thought that there was anything spiritual or of a saving nature in this.

From about that time I began to have a new kind of understanding of Christ and the work of redemption and the glorious way of salvation by Him. An inward, sweet sense of these things at times came into my heart. My soul was led away in pleasant views and contemplations of them. And my mind was greatly engaged to spend my time in reading and meditating on Christ, on the beauty and excellency of His person and the lovely way of salvation by free grace in Him. I found no books so delightful to me as those that spoke of these subjects.

Those words in Song of Songs 2:1 used to be abundantly with me, "I am the rose of Sharon, and the lily of the valleys." The words seemed to me to sweetly represent the loveliness and beauty of Jesus Christ. The whole book of Song of Songs was pleasant to me, and I was very engaged in reading it. I found from time to time an inward sweetness that would carry me away in my contemplations. I do not know how to express this other than by a calm, sweet preoccupation of soul from all the concerns of this world. At other times I would have fixed ideas and imaginations of being alone in the mountains or some solitary wilderness far from all mankind, sweetly conversing with Christ and wrapt and swallowed up in God. The sense I had of divine things would often suddenly kindle up, as it were, a sweet burning in my heart, a passion of soul, that I know not how to express.

Not long after I first began to experience these things, I gave an account to my father of some things that had passed in my mind. I was pretty much affected by the conversation we had together. When it was ended, I walked alone in a solitary place in my father's pasture for contemplation. And as I was walking there and looking upon the sky and clouds, there came into my mind so sweet a sense of the glorious *majesty* and *grace* of God that I do not know how to express. I seemed to see them both in a sweet conjunction — majesty and meekness joined together. It was a sweet and gentle and holy majesty; and also a majestic meekness, an awful sweetness, a high and great and holy gentleness.

After this my sense of divine things gradually increased and became more and more lively and had more of that inward sweetness. The appearance of everything was altered. There seemed to be a calm, sweet cast or appearance of divine glory in almost everything. God's excellency, His wisdom, His purity, and love seemed to appear in everything — in the sun, moon, and stars; in the clouds and blue sky; in the grass, flowers, and trees; in the water and all nature — which used to greatly hold my attention.

I often used to sit and view the moon for a long time. In the day, I spent much time in viewing the clouds and sky to behold the sweet glory of God in these things. In the meantime I would sing forth, with a low voice, my contemplations of the Creator and Redeemer. There was scarcely nothing among all the works of nature that was so sweet to me as thunder and lightning. Before, I used to be uncommonly terrified with thunder and struck with terror when I saw a thunderstorm rising. But now, on the contrary, it made me rejoice! I felt God, if I may so speak, at the first appearance of a thunderstorm, and used to take the opportunity to position myself in order to view the clouds, see the lightnings play, and hear the majestic and awful voice of God's thunders. These things were often exceedingly entertaining, leading me to sweet contemplations of my great and glorious God. While engaged in this way, it always seemed natural for me to sing or chant forth my meditations or to speak my thoughts in soliloquies with a singing voice.

I felt then great satisfaction about my good estate, but that did not content me. I had intense longings of soul after God and Christ and after more holiness. My heart seemed to be full and ready to break, which often brought to my mind the words of the Psalmist in Psalm 119:28: "My soul breaks for the longing it has." I often felt a mourning and lamenting in my heart that I had not turned to God sooner so that I might have had more time to grow in grace. My mind was greatly fixed on divine things and almost perpetually contemplating them. I spent most of my time in thinking of divine things year after year. I often walked alone in the woods and solitary places for meditation, soliloquy, and prayer, fellowshipping with God. It was always my manner at such times to sing forth my contemplations. I was almost constantly releasing short prayers wherever I was. Prayer seemed to be natural to me, as the breath by which the inward burnings of my heart had vent.

The delights that I now felt in the things of religion were of an exceedingly different kind from those before-mentioned. When I was a boy, I had no more knowledge of these delights than one born blind has of pleasant and beautiful colors. These delights were of a more inward, pure, soul-animating, and refreshing nature. Those former delights never reached the heart and did not arise from any sight of the divine excellency of the things of God or any taste of the soul-satisfying and life-giving good there is in them. [1]

Jonathan Edwards was transferred from a most miserable state to a state of sweetness. The Bible describes this transfer in the life of every miserable person who will let go of their misery and let Christ in. Ephesians 2:2-3 defines *the misery under sin:* [2] "In which you once walked according to the course of this world, according to the prince of the power of the air, the spirit who now works in the sons of disobedience, [3] among whom also we all once conducted ourselves in the lusts of our flesh, fulfilling the desires of the flesh and of the mind, and were by nature children of wrath, just as the others." Then verses 4-5 describe *the sweetness in Christ:* [4] "But

God, who is rich in mercy, because of His great love with which He loved us, [5] even when we were dead in trespasses, made us alive together with Christ (by grace you have been saved)."

The sweetness of God's mercy, love, and grace over us in our dead and miserable condition is backed up by the power of His life. He comes in and changes us from within by giving us a new spirit and a new heart. He will take away the misery of our "heart of stone" and, as He did in Jonathan Edwards, give us "a heart of flesh," that is, a heart with feeling and love for God in it (Ezek. 36:26). He does it all in us. It is this inner miracle that God works in the heart that will call forth those same words — "sweet! Oh, the sweetness of such a Christ!"

8 George Whitefield

· A Religious Life ·

"I know the place…
whenever I go to Oxford
I cannot help running
to the spot where Jesus
Christ first revealed
Himself to me and
gave me the new birth."

(1714-1770)

A s a teenager, George Whitefield desired to live a
*religious and serious life. He engaged in numerous
religious exercises such as fasting, praying regularly,
attending public worship, and abstaining from worldly
pleasures. However, it was not until Charles Wesley
gave him Henry Scougal's book* The Life of God in the
Soul of Man *that he saw that he had never personally
found Christ. A ray of divine light darted in upon his soul
when he realized that "true religion was union of the
soul with God, and Christ formed within us."* [1]

*After this experience, Whitefield became one of the
most effective preachers of the gospel that the church has
known. His trips to America were largely responsible for
the first Great Awakening, which took place in the mid-
eighteenth century. The following is Whitefield's testi-*

mony about how he found Christ. It is taken from his
journal and a sermon he preached later in his life.

BEING NOW NEAR seventeen years of age, I was
resolved to prepare myself for the holy sacrament,
which I received on Christmas day. I began to be more
and more watchful over my thoughts, words, and actions. I observed the following Lent, fasting Wednesday
and Friday for thirty-six hours. My evenings, when I was
done waiting upon my mother, were generally spent in
acts of devotion, reading *Drelincourt on Death* and other
practical books. And I regularly went to public worship
twice a day. Being now an upperclassman, by God's help
I made some reformation among my schoolfellows. I
was very diligent in reading and learning the classics and
in studying my Greek Testament, but was not yet convinced of the absolute unlawfulness of playing cards and
of reading and seeing plays, though I began to have some
question marks about it.

Near this time I dreamed that I was to see God on
Mount Sinai, but was afraid to meet Him. This made a
great impression upon me, and a gentlewoman to whom
I told it, said, "George, this is a call from God." I grew
still more serious after this dream. Yet hypocrisy crept
into every action. As I once feigned to look more fash-
ionable, I now strove to appear more grave than I really
was. However, an uncommon concern and change was

visible in my behavior, and I often used to find fault with the lightness of others.

One night as I was going on an errand for my mother, an unaccountable but very strong impression was made upon my heart that I would be preaching very soon. When I came home, I innocently told my mother what had happened to me. But she, like Joseph's parents, when he told them his dream, scolded me, crying out, "What does the boy mean? I pray thee hold thy tongue," or something to that effect. God has since shown her from Whom that impression came.

For a year I went on in a round of duties, receiving the sacrament monthly, fasting frequently, attending public worship constantly, and praying often more than twice a day in private. One of my brothers used to tell me that he feared this would not last long and that I would forget all when I came to Oxford. This caution did me much service, for it set me upon praying for perseverance. And, under God, the preparation I made in the country was a preservative against the many temptations which came upon me at my first arriving at that seat of learning.

Being now near eighteen years old, it was judged proper for me to go to the University. God had sweetly prepared my way. Some friends of mine recommended me to the Master of Pembroke College. Another friend loaned me 10 pounds, which I have since repaid, to defray the first expense of entering. And the Master, contrary to all expectations, admitted me immediately as a servitor.[‡]

Soon after my admission I went and resided at Pembroke College. At that time many of the servitors were sick. Due to my diligent and ready attendance, I found favor with the fellows, and many chose me to be their servitor. This greatly lessened my expense, and indeed, God was so gracious, that with the profits of my service and some small gifts given to me by my kind tutor, I did not require from my family more than 24 pounds for expenses for almost the first three years. And it has often grieved my soul to see so many young students spending their substance in extravagant living and entirely unfitting themselves for the pursuing of their studies.

I had not been long at the University before I found the benefit of the foundation I had laid in the country for a holy life. I was quickly invited to join in their excess of riot with several who slept in the same room. God, in answer to previous prayers, gave me grace to withstand them. One night in particular, it was very cold. Because I would not go out and join them but remained alone in my study, my limbs became so numb that I could scarcely sleep all night. But I soon found the benefit of not yielding. For when they perceived they could not prevail, they left me alone as a singular odd fellow.

[‡] An undergraduate selected to serve "the fellows" at the University in order to pay for his expenses.

All this happened to me, yet I was still not fully convicted of the sin of playing cards and reading plays, until God on a day of fasting was pleased to convince me. For, taking a play to read a passage out of it to a friend, God struck my heart with such power that I was compelled to lay it down again. And, blessed be His Name, I have not read any such book since.

Before I went to the University, I was introduced to William Law's *Serious Call to a Devout Life,* but did not have the money to purchase it. However, soon after my arrival at the University, I saw a small edition of it in a friend's hand and soon obtained a copy of my own. God worked powerfully upon my soul, as He has since upon many others, by that book, as well as Mr. Law's other excellent treatise on *Christian Perfection.*

I now began to pray and sing psalms three times every day, besides morning and evening. I also fasted every Friday and received the sacrament at a parish church near our college, and at the castle, where the so-called "despised Methodists" used to receive it once a month. These young men were much talked about at Oxford. I had heard of them, and loved them before I came to the University. Indeed, I so strenuously defended them when I heard them reviled by the students, that they began to think that I also in time should be one of them.

For more than a year my soul longed to be acquainted

with some of them. I was strongly pressed to follow their good example when I saw them go through a ridiculing crowd to receive the holy sacrament at St. Mary's. The time came when God was pleased to open a door. It happened that a poor woman in one of the workhouses had attempted to cut her throat, but was happily prevented. Upon hearing of this, and knowing that both John and Charles Wesley were ready to every good work, I sent a poor apple-woman of our college to inform Charles Wesley of it, charging her not to tell who sent her. She went, but contrary to my orders, told my name. Charles, having previously heard of my coming to the castle and a parish-church sacrament, and having met me frequently walking by myself, followed the woman when she left and sent an invitation to me by her to come to breakfast with him the next morning.

I thankfully embraced the opportunity. Blessed be God! it was one of the most profitable visits I ever had in my life. My soul, at that time, was longing for some spiritual friends to lift up my hands when they hung down and to strengthen my feeble knees. He soon discovered it and, like a wise winner of souls, made all his conversations tend that way. And when he had given me Professor Francke's book *Against the Fear of Man* and a book entitled *The Country Parson's Advice to His Parishioners* (the last of which was wonderfully blessed to my soul) I left him.

In a short time he let me have another book entitled *The Life of God in the Soul of Man.* And though I had fasted, watched and prayed, and received the sacrament so long, yet I never knew what true religion was, until God sent me that excellent treatise by the hands of my never-to-be-forgotten friend, Charles Wesley.

At my first reading it, I wondered what the author meant by saying, "Some falsely placed religion in going to church, doing harm to no one, being constant in their private devotions, and now and then reaching out their hands to give alms to their poor neighbors." "Alas!" I thought, "if this be not true religion, what is?" God soon showed me. For in reading a few lines further that "true religion was union of the soul with God, and Christ formed within us," a ray of divine light was instantaneously darted in upon my soul, and from that moment, but not until then, did I know that I must be a new creature.

Now, like the woman of Samaria, when Christ revealed Himself to her at the well, I had no rest in my soul until I wrote letters to my relatives, telling them there was such a thing as the new birth. I thought they would gladly receive it. But, alas! my words seemed to them as idle tales. They thought that I was beside myself, and by their letters confirmed my own resolutions not to go down into the country. Instead, I would continue where I was so that, by any means, the good work that God had begun in my soul would not be made of none effect.

From time to time Mr. Wesley permitted me to come to him and instructed me as I was able to receive it. By degrees he introduced me to the rest of his Christian brethren. They built me up daily in the knowledge and fear of God, and taught me to endure hardness like a good soldier of Jesus Christ. [2]

Much later in his life, in a sermon of 1769, Whitefield again bore witness to the same great experience:

I must bear testimony to my old friend Mr. Charles Wesley. He put a book into my hands called *The Life of God in the Soul of Man,* through which God showed me that I must be born again or be damned. I know the place. It may perhaps sound superstitious, but whenever I go to Oxford I cannot help running to the spot where Jesus Christ first revealed Himself to me and gave me the new birth. I learned that a man may go to church, say his prayers, and receive the sacrament, and yet not be a Christian. How my heart did rise and shudder like a poor man who is most reluctant to look into his ledger for fear that he would find himself bankrupt. "Shall I burn this book? Shall I throw it down? or shall I search it?" I did search it and, holding the book in my hand, thus addressed the God of heaven and earth, "Lord, if I am not a Christian, for Jesus Christ's sake show me what Christianity is, that I may not be damned at last." I read a little further and discovered that they who know anything of religion know it is a vital union with the Son of God — Christ formed in the heart. O what a ray of divine life did then break in upon my soul!

I began writing to all my brethren and to my sisters. I talked to the students as they came into my room. I laid aside all frivolous conversation. I put all shallow books away and was determined to study to be a saint, and then to be a scholar. From that moment God has been carrying on His blessed work in my soul. I am now fifty-five years of age and shall leave you in a few days. But I tell you, my brethren, I am more and more convinced that this is the truth of God, and that without it you can never be saved by Jesus Christ.[3]

———————————◆———————————

It is not uncommon for a moral person like George Whitefield, who mistakenly places his hope in mere religious practices, to one day suddenly discover that what pleases God is not man's efforts, but a new birth that brings one into union with Christ. This was the apostle Paul's testimony in Galatians 1:14-16: [14]"And I advanced in Judaism beyond many of my contemporaries in my own nation, being more exceedingly zealous for the traditions of my fathers. [15]But when *it pleased God,* who separated me from my mother's womb and called me through His grace, [16]*to reveal His Son in me.*"

If you are a person striving religiously within yourself to please God, you need to see that what God wants from you is that you receive Christ, are joined to Him, and have a new birth now. The way for this to happen to you is given clearly in John 1:12-13: [12] "But as many as *received Him,* to them He gave the right to become children of God, even to those who believe in His name: [13] who were born, not of blood, nor of the will of the flesh, nor of the will of man, but of God."

To receive Christ and believe in His name is a simple act of faith from your heart and with your mouth. Just open your heart and call upon His name — "Lord Jesus." You receive Him the moment you open and call. This gives the Lord the way to actually come into you so that you might be born of God and be in union with Him. "The one who joins himself to the Lord is *one spirit* with Him" (1 Cor. 6:17, NASV). As soon as you take this step, a ray of divine light will instantaneously dart in upon your soul, for Romans 8:16 tells us, "The Spirit Himself bears witness with our spirit that *we are* children of God."

9 Charles Finney

• A Proud Heart •

"I saw that His work was
a finished work and that
instead of having any
righteousness of my own
to recommend me to God,
I had to submit myself to
the righteousness of God
through Christ."

(1792-1875)

Charles Finney was a young attorney practicing law in Adams, New York, when he began to seek after the salvation of his soul. He found that the most troublesome hindrance for him in seeking God was his pride and fear of men — he was ashamed to be found reading the Bible or praying.

In 1821 while praying secretly in the woods, he found Christ and received "a retainer from the Lord to plead His cause." His shame disappeared and Finney began a ministry of revival preaching that brought an estimated half million people to Christ. This was an amazing accomplishment in a day without loudspeakers and mass communication. The following excerpt is from his memoirs and describes how he found Christ.

O N A SABBATH EVENING in the autumn of 1821, I made up my mind that I would settle the question of my soul's salvation at once, that if it were possible I would make my peace with God. But because I was very busy in the affairs of the office, I knew that without great firmness of purpose, I would never effectually attend to the subject. I therefore, then and there resolved, as far as possible, to avoid all business and everything that would divert my attention, and to give myself wholly to the work of securing the salvation of my soul. I carried out this resolution as sternly and thoroughly as I could. I was, however, required to be a good deal in the office. But as the providence of God would have it, I was not very occupied either on Monday or Tuesday and had opportunity to read my Bible and engage in prayer most of the time.

But I was very proud without knowing it. I had supposed that I had not much regard for the opinions of others, whether they thought this or that in regard to myself. And in fact I had been quite faithful in attending prayer meetings and had paid some degree of attention to religion while in Adams. In this respect I had been so singular as to lead the church at times to think that I must be an anxious inquirer. But I found, when I came to face the question, that I was very unwilling to have anyone know that I was seeking the salvation of my soul. When I prayed I would only whisper my prayer, after plugging the keyhole to the door, so that no one would discover that I was engaged in prayer. Before that time I had my Bible lying on the table with the lawbooks. It never had occurred to me to be ashamed of being found reading it, anymore than I should be ashamed of being found reading any of my other books.

But after I had earnestly resolved to seek my own salvation, I kept my Bible, as much as I could, out of sight. If I was reading it when anyone came in, I would throw my lawbooks upon it to create the impression that I had not had it in my hand. Instead of being outspoken and willing to talk with anyone and everyone on the subject as before, I found myself unwilling to converse with anyone. I did not want to see my minister because I did not want to let him know how I felt, and I had no confidence that he would understand my case and give me the direction that I needed. For the same reasons I avoided conversation with the elders of the church or with any of the Christian people. I was ashamed to let them know how I felt, on the one hand; and on the other, I was afraid they would misdirect me. I felt myself shut up to the Bible.

During Monday and Tuesday my convictions in-creased, but still it seemed as if my heart grew harder. I could not shed a tear. I could not pray. I had no opportu-nity to pray above my breath. And frequently I felt that if I could be alone where I could use my voice and let myself out, I would find relief in prayer. I was shy and I avoided, as much as I could, speaking to anyone on any subject. I endeavored, however, to do this in a way that would excite no suspicion, in any mind, that I was seeking the salvation of my soul.

Tuesday night I had become very nervous, and in the night a strange feeling came over me as if I was about to die. I knew that if I did I would sink down to hell. But I quieted myself as best I could until morning.

At an early hour I started for the office. But just before I arrived, something seemed to confront me with questions. Indeed, it seemed as if the inquiry was within myself, as if an inward voice said to me, "What are you waiting for? Did you not promise to give your heart to God? And what are you trying to do? Are you endeavoring to work out a righteousness of your own?"

Just at this point the whole question of gospel salvation opened to my mind in a most marvelous way. I think I then saw, as clearly as I ever have in my life, the reality and fullness of the atonement of Christ. I saw that His work was a finished work and that instead of having or needing any righteousness of my own to recommend me to God, I had to submit myself to the righteousness of God through Christ. Gospel salvation seemed to me to be an offer of something to be accepted. It was full and complete, and all that was necessary on my part was to get my own consent to give up my sins and accept Christ.

Salvation, it seemed to me, instead of being a thing to be wrought out by my own works, was a thing to be found entirely in the Lord Jesus Christ, who presented Himself before me as my God and my Savior.

Without being distinctly aware of it, I had stopped in the street right where the inward voice seemed to arrest me. How long I remained in that position I cannot say. But after this distinct revelation had stood before my mind for some time, the question seemed to be put, "Will you accept it now, today?" I replied, "Yes, I will accept it today, or I will die in the attempt."

North of the village and over a hill lay a piece of woods, in which I was in the almost daily habit of walking when it was pleasant weather. It was now October, and the time was past for my frequent walks there. Nevertheless, instead of going to the office, I turned and bent my course toward the woods, feeling that I must be alone and away from all human eyes and ears so that I could pour out my prayer to God.

But still my pride must show itself. As I went over the hill, it occurred to me that someone might see me and suppose that I was going away to pray. Yet probably there was not a person on earth that would have suspected such a thing had he seen me going. But so great was my pride and so much was I possessed with the fear of man that I recall sneaking along under the fence until I got so far out of sight that no one from the village could see me. I then penetrated into the woods about a quarter of a mile, went over on the other side of the hill and found a place where some large trees had fallen across each other, leaving an open place between. There I saw I could make a kind of closet. I crept into this place and knelt down for prayer. As I turned to go up into the woods, I recall that I said, "I will give my heart to God, or I never will come down from there." I remember repeating this as I went up — "I will give my heart to God before I ever come down again."

But when I attempted to pray I found that my heart would not pray. I had supposed that if I could only be where I could speak aloud without being overheard, I could pray freely. But lo! when I came to try, I was dumb. I had nothing to say to God, or at least I could say but a few words, and those without heart. In attempting to pray I would hear a rustling in the leaves, as I thought, and would stop and look up to see if someone was coming. This I did several times.

Finally I found myself quickly on the verge of despair. I said to myself, "I cannot pray. My heart is dead to God and will not pray." I then reproached myself for having promised to give my heart to God before I left the woods. When I came to try, I found I could not give my heart to God. My inward soul hung back, and there was no going out of my heart to God. I began to feel deeply that it was too late, that it must be that God had given up on me and I was past hope.

The thought was pressing me of the rashness of my promise, that I would give my heart to God that day or die in the attempt. It seemed to me as if that was binding upon my soul, and yet I was going to break my vow. A great sinking and discouragement came over me, and I felt almost too weak to stand upon my knees.

Just at this moment I again thought I heard someone approach me, and I opened my eyes to see if it was so. But right there the revelation of my pride of heart, as the great difficulty that stood in the way, was distinctly shown to me. An overwhelming sense of my wickedness, in being ashamed to have a human being see me on my knees before God, took such powerful possession of me that I cried at the top of my voice and exclaimed that I would not leave that place if all the men on earth and all the devils in hell surrounded me. "What!" I said, "such a degraded sinner as I am, on my knees confessing my sins to the great and holy God, and ashamed to have any human being, and a sinner like myself, find me on my knees endeavoring to make my peace with my offended God!" The sin appeared awful, infinite. It broke me down before the Lord.

Just at that point, this passage of Scripture seemed to drop into my mind with a flood of light: "Then shall you go and pray unto Me, and I will hear you. Then shall you seek Me and find Me, when you shall search for Me with all your heart." I instantly seized hold of this with my heart. I had intellectually believed the Bible before, but never had the truth been in my mind that faith was a voluntary trust instead of an intellectual state. At that moment I was as conscious of trusting in God's veracity as I was of my own existence. Somehow I knew that that was a passage of Scripture, though I do not think I had ever read it. I knew that it was God's word, and God's voice, as it were, that spoke to me. I cried to Him, "Lord, I take You at Your word. Now You know that I do search for You with all my heart and that I have come here to pray to You, and You have promised to hear me."

That seemed to settle the question that I could then, that day, perform my vow. The Spirit seemed to lay stress upon that idea in the text, "When you search for Me with all your heart." The question of when, that is, of the present time, seemed to fall heavily into my heart. I told the Lord that I would take Him at His word, that He could not lie, and that therefore I was sure that He heard my prayer and would be found of me.

He then gave me many other promises, both from the Old and the New Testament, especially some most precious promises concerning our Lord Jesus Christ. I never can, in words, make any human being understand how precious and true those promises appeared to me. I took them one after the other as infallible truth, the assertions of God who could not lie. They did not seem so much to fall into my intellect as into my heart, to be put within the grasp of the voluntary powers of my mind. I seized hold of them, appropriated them, and fastened upon them with the grasp of a drowning man.

I continued thus to pray and to receive and appropriate promises for a long time, how long I do not know. I prayed until my mind became so full that, before I was aware of it, I was on my feet and tripping up the ascent toward the road. The question of my being converted had not so much as arisen to my thought. But as I went up, brushing through the leaves and bushes, I recalled that I had said with great emphasis "If I am ever converted, I will preach the Gospel." [1]

◆

The obstacle that many people face in coming to Christ is their pride. Like Charles Finney, you may have wanted to receive Christ, but your pride has hindered you. However, when Finney saw the pride of his heart, it created in him a greater sense of need for God, and it was at that point that he searched for Him with *all* of his heart and found Him.

Don't be dismayed. The Bible has a specific word for a proud person: [6] "God resists the proud, but gives grace to the humble. [7] Therefore *submit* to God. Resist the devil and he will flee from you. [8] *Draw near* to God and He will draw near to you. *Cleanse* your hands, you sinners; and *purify* your hearts, you double-minded" (James 4:6-8).

The way to break through your pride is simply to humble yourself and pray like the sinful tax collector did in Luke 18:13-14: [13] "And the tax collector, standing afar off, would not so much as raise his eyes to heaven, but beat his breast, saying, *'God be merciful to me a sinner!'* [14] I tell you, this man went down to his house justified rather than the other [the proud Pharisee]; for everyone who exalts himself will be abased, and he who humbles himself will be exalted." What are you waiting for? Do it now. "Behold, *now* is the acceptable time; behold, *now* is the day of salvation" (2 Cor. 6:2).

Christ is waiting at the door of your heart to come in, so there is only one thing for you to do — *open* the door and He will come in: "Behold, I stand at the door and knock. If anyone hears My voice and opens the door, I will come in to him and dine with him, and he with Me" (Rev. 3:20).

10 George Müller

· Indifference toward God ·

"When I was as
careless about Him
as ever, He sent His
Spirit into my heart."

(1805-1898)

A *s a young man, George Müller lived a sinful and
dissipated life. Because his indulgence in sinful
pleasures occupied his time and heart, his attitude
toward God was one of general indifference. However,
while attending the University of Halle, he came into
contact with a number of Christians who made a deep
impression on him. He himself soon found Christ, which
became the turning point of his life.*

*In the years that followed, Müller's life of faith and
prayers became a great inspiration to Christians and
has continued to be to this day. The unique testimony of
his life was that he established five large orphan homes
during the nineteenth century, in which more than ten
thousand children were completely cared for over a
period of sixty-two years. More than seven million*

dollars passed through Müller's hands for the care of the orphans, without his asking for a single penny from man. He relied solely on faith and prayer to supply all the needs. The following is taken from his autobiography and includes the period leading up to his conversion experience:

I WAS BORN at Kroppenstaedt, near Halberstadt, in the kingdom of Prussia, on September 27th, 1805. My father, who educated his children on worldly principles, gave us much money, considering our age; not in order that we might spend it, but, as he said, to accustom us to possess money without spending it. The result was that it led me and my brother into many sins.

When I was between ten and eleven years of age, I was sent to Halberstadt, to the Cathedral Classical School, there to be prepared for the University. My father's desire was that I should become a clergyman, not that I might serve God, but that I might have a comfortable living. My time was now spent in studying, reading novels, and indulging, though so young, in sinful practices. Thus it continued until I was fourteen years old.

I grew worse and worse. Three or four days before I was confirmed (and thus admitted to partake of the Lord's supper), I was guilty of gross immorality. And the very day before my confirmation, when I was in the vestry with the clergyman to confess my sins (according to the usual practice), I defrauded him, for I handed over to him only the twelfth part of the fee which my father had given me for him.

In this state of heart, without prayer, without true repentance, without faith, without knowledge of the plan of salvation, I was confirmed and took the Lord's supper on the Sunday after Easter, 1820. I also made resolutions to turn from those vices in which I was living and to study more. But as I attempted the thing in my own strength, all soon came to nothing, and I still grew worse.

I became a member of the University and obtained permission to preach in the Lutheran Establishment, but I was as truly unhappy and as far from God as ever. I had made strong resolutions, now at last to change my course of life, for two reasons: first, because without it I thought no parish would choose me as their pastor; and secondly, that without a considerable knowledge of divinity I would never get a good living, because the obtaining of a valuable assignment in Prussia generally depends upon the degree which the candidates for the ministry obtain in passing the examination. But the moment I entered Halle, the University town, all my resolutions came to nothing.

At this time, in September 1825, Halle was frequented by 1,260 students, about 900 of whom studied divinity, all of which 900 were allowed to preach, although, I believe, not nine of them feared the Lord.

The time had now come when God would have mercy upon me. His love had been set upon such a wretch as I was before the world was made. His love had sent His Son to bear punishment on account of my sins, and to fulfill the law which I had broken times without number. And now at a time when I was as careless about Him as ever, He sent His Spirit into my heart. I had no Bible, and had not read it for years. I seldom went to church; but, from custom, I took the Lord's supper twice a year. I had never heard the gospel preached up to the beginning of November 1825. I had never met a person who told me that he meant, by the help of God, to live according to the Holy Scriptures. In short, I had not the least idea that there were any persons really different from myself, except in degree.

One Saturday afternoon, about the middle of November 1825, I had taken a walk with my friend Beta. On our return he said to me that he was in the habit of going on Saturday evenings to the house of a Christian, where there was a meeting. On further inquiry he told me that they read the Bible, sang, prayed, and read a printed sermon. No sooner had I heard this, than it was to me as if I had found something after which I had been seeking all my life long. I immediately wished to go with my friend, who at first was not willing to take me. For knowing me to be a lively young man, he thought I would not like this meeting. At last, however, he said he would come for me.

I would here mention that Beta seems to have had conviction of sin, and probably also a degree of acquaintance with the Lord, when about fifteen years old. Afterwards, being in a cold and worldly state, he joined me in a sinful journey to Switzerland. When he returned, however, being extremely miserable and convinced of his guilt, he made a full confession of his sin to his father; and while with him, sought the acquaintance of a Christian brother named Richter. This Dr. Richter gave him, on his return to the University, a letter of introduction to a believing tradesman by the name of Wagner. It was this brother in whose house the meeting was held.

We went together in the evening. As I did not know the manners of believers, and the joy they have in seeing poor sinners even in any measure caring about the things of God, I made an apology for coming. The kind answer of this dear brother I shall never forget. He said, "Come as often as you please; house and heart are open to you." We sat down and sang a hymn. Then brother Kayser, afterwards a missionary in Africa in connection with the London Missionary Society, who was then living at Halle, fell on his knees, and asked a blessing on our meeting. This kneeling down made a deep impression upon me; for I had never either seen anyone on his knees, nor had I ever prayed myself on my knees. He then read a chapter and a printed sermon, for no regular meetings for expounding the Scriptures were allowed in Prussia unless an ordained clergyman was present. At the close we sang another hymn, and then the master of the house prayed. While he prayed, my feeling was something like this: I could not pray as well, though I am much more learned than this illiterate man. The whole meeting made a deep impression on me. I was happy, though if I had been asked why, I could not have clearly explained it.

When we walked home, I said to Beta, "All we have seen on our journey to Switzerland, and all our former pleasures, are as nothing in comparison with this evening." Whether I fell on my knees when I returned home, I do not remember; but this I know, that I lay peaceful and happy in my bed. This shows that the Lord may begin His work in different ways. For I have not the least doubt that on that evening He began a work of grace in me, though I obtained joy without any deep sorrow of heart, and with scarcely any knowledge. That evening was the turning point in my life. The next day, and Monday, and once or twice besides, I went again to the house of this brother, where I read the Scriptures with him and another brother; for it was too long for me to wait until Saturday came again.

Now my life became very different, though all sins were not given up at once. My wicked companions were given up. The going to taverns was entirely discontinued. The habitual practice of telling falsehoods was no longer indulged in, but still a few times after this I spoke an untruth. At the time when this change took place, I was engaged in translating a novel out of French into German for the press, in order to obtain the means of gratifying my desire to see Paris. This plan about the journey was now given up, though I had not enough of God's light to give up the work in which I was engaged, but finished it. The Lord, however, most remarkably put various obstacles in the way and did not allow me to sell the manuscript. At last, seeing that *the whole* was wrong, I determined never to sell it, and was enabled to abide by this determination. The manuscript was burnt.

I now no longer lived habitually in sin, though I was still often overcome, and sometimes even by open sins, though far less frequently than before, and not without sorrow of heart. I read the Scriptures, prayed often, loved the brethren, went to church from right motives, and stood on the side of Christ, though laughed at by my fellow students.

What all the exhortations and precepts of my father and others could not effect, what all my own resolutions could not bring about — even to renounce a life of sin and profligacy — I was enabled to do, constrained by the love of Jesus. The individual who desires to have his sins forgiven must seek for it through the blood of Jesus. The individual who desires to get power over sin must likewise seek it through the blood of Jesus. [1]

———————————◆———————————

Often God makes Himself known to a person when they are in a condition of careless indifference. This was the case with George Müller. In your own life you may not have been that concerned about your relationship with God, but for some unknown reason your interest has been drawn toward spiritual things. Perhaps a friend or an unexpected turn of events or a message you heard has caused you to reflect on God, and you are now thinking about becoming a Christian.

You should realize that this kind of inward activity *is* the working of the Holy Spirit in your life. Notice how Jesus describes what happens to a person when he is born again: "The wind blows where it wishes, and you hear the sound of it, but cannot tell where it comes from and where it goes. So is everyone who is born of the Spirit" (John 3:8). This means that something is happening to you, yet you are not sure why it is happening. You are just mysteriously drawn to God. At this point in your life you must recognize that Christ is closer to you than you thought.

Jesus said, "No one can come to Me unless the Father who sent Me draws him" (John 6:44). Your feelings of being drawn to the Lord must be understood not as a passing emotion but as God Himself bringing you to Christ. Your part is simply to respond to this drawing by receiving the gift of God, which is eternal life through Jesus Christ our Lord (Rom. 6:23). To receive this gift you need only to pray from your heart the following suggested prayer: "Lord Jesus, I am a sinner and I confess my sins to You. I believe that You died on the cross and shed Your blood for me. I accept Your forgiveness, and I open myself and receive You now as my Savior and Life. Thank You for coming into me. I do believe that You have given me the gift of eternal life and that You now live in me. I do believe in Your Name and confess with my mouth, Lord Jesus! Amen!"

11 Andrew Murray

• An Impacted Life •

"I am confident that
as a sinner I have
been led to cast
myself on Christ."

(1828-1917)

*A*ndrew Murray has become a household name to
multitudes of seeking Christians for well over a
century. His life and ministry continue to speak with
spiritual power through his many writings. His classic
work, With Christ in the School of Prayer, *has been one
of the chief influences behind many of the revivals of the
last one hundred years.*

*The main factors that led to Andrew Murray's salva-
tion at age seventeen include "the blessing of praying
parents" and the deep spiritual impressions he received
from godly men and women who impacted his life during
the years of his formal education in Scotland and Holland.*

*After leaving South Africa, where he was born,
Andrew and his brother first spent seven years in Aberdeen, Scotland, and then three years in Utrecht, Holland.*

While he was in Scotland in his formative years, Andrew came under the influence of many men of God, including Thomas Chalmers, Robert S. Candlish, Robert Murray McCheyne, Andrew and Horatius Bonar, and William C. Burns. The most instrumental in his life in those years was Burns, who was also mightily used of God to bring revival throughout Scotland. Burns later went to China and had a profound impact upon Hudson Taylor as well.

One of the early seeds sown into Andrew's heart to lead him to Christ was a pointed letter written by Burns to Andrew's brother John, with a P.S. to Andrew. The content of the letter is as follows:

"Forsake not the works of thine own hands." Psa. 138:8
DUNDEE, 13th January, 1841.

MY DEAR FRIEND, I was happy to receive your interesting letter, and I have been attempting in the all-prevailing name of Jesus to commend your soul in its present affecting case to the infinitely merciful and gracious Jehovah. Do not, I beseech you, give way to the secret thought that you are excusable in remaining in your present unrenewed state, or that there is the smallest possible hope of your being saved unless you are really born of the Holy Spirit, and reconciled to the Holy Jehovah by the atoning blood of His only-begotten Son. Search your heart, my dear fellow-sinner, and I am sure that you will find something which you are refusing to let go at the command of

God, and look upon this secret reserve in your surrender to Him as the reason on account of which He seems for a time to overlook your case. He is a God of infinite holiness, and cannot look upon iniquity. If we regard iniquity in our heart the Lord will not hear us. But if you are coming in sincerity of heart to Him through Jesus Christ, you will find Him to be a God of infinite mercy and loving-kindness, delighting in mercy and having no pleasure in the death of the sinner. Do not doubt, as your own wicked heart, under the power of Satan, would tempt you to do, that there is mercy for you if you do not willingly harden your heart against Jehovah's voice of authority and love. He will make Himself known to you in good time. Wait on Him. I can testify this to you from my own experience. Often do I think that God has forgotten me, but I find that afterwards He answers prayers which I have forgotten. Oh! dear friend, be not tempted to put off to a more convenient season your entire consecration to Emmanuel. You are enjoying in Jehovah's infinite and most undeserved mercy a convenient season at present; oh! improve it, lest the great God should be provoked and swear in His wrath, "You shall not enter into My rest." I will continue to pray for you, and I have hope in the Lord that I may be heard for His own glory. Jesus' service and His presence are indeed sweet.

I am, dear John,

Your affectionate friend in the Lord Jesus,

Wm. C. BURNS.

P.S. — Show this to Andrew, whom it may also suit. I got his letter and shall answer it afterwards if the Lord will. Write me again. [1]

The content of Burns's letter reveals that he discerned that both John and Andrew needed to be born of the Holy Spirit. There were many other encounters like this in Scotland — all preparing Andrew to find Christ. After seven years in that country, he and his brother went to Utrecht, Holland, to prepare for the ministry.

The spiritual condition in Holland was deplorable. Andrew found himself in the midst of rationalism, liberalism, and a dead and indifferent professing church that was steeped in outward religious forms without any heart or life. This caused Andrew to begin seeking the Lord in a new way. At this time in the city of Utrecht, a small group of students were forming a club called Sechor Dabar *("Remember the Word"). Andrew and John Murray became core members of this group. The intent and practice of this club was similar to the "Holy Club" that was formed a century before at Oxford under the Wesleys.*

The students of Sechor Dabar *were touched by the revival movement coming out of Geneva, Switzerland, under the leadership of Robert and James Haldane. This movement was called* Réveil, *the French word for* revival, *and included such names as Merle d'Aubigné and Frédéric Monod.*

Sechor Dabar *met once a week and took a firm stand against the worldliness of the other professing ministerial students and suffered ridicule because of this. They drank only tea and coffee and ate chocolate, refusing wine and liquors. They were derisively nicknamed "The Chocolate Club" and "The Prayer Club" by both students and professors.*

During this period, Andrew was spending nights mapping out his week so that he would have definite and fixed duties for every moment of the day. Within Andrew the impact of all the previous years of spiritual impressions and godly influences and experiences came to a head in his heart. As he reflected on all these things, the stumbling block in his mind was removed concerning what was necessary for him to be saved. This event, along with being exposed to the degraded atmosphere of the professing Christian world, brought Andrew to a distinct surrender to Christ. He expresses this experience in a letter to his parents:

Utrecht, 14th November, 1845.
My Dear Parents,

IT WAS WITH VERY great pleasure that I today received your letter of 15th August, containing the announcement of the birth of another brother. And equal, I am sure, will be your delight when I tell you that I can communicate to you far gladder tidings, over which angels have rejoiced, that your son has been born again. It would be difficult for me to express what I feel on writing to you on this subject. Always up to now in my letters, and even yet in my conversation, there has been stiffness in speaking about such things, and even now I hardly know how I shall write.

When I look back to see how I have been brought to where I now am, I must acknowledge that I see nothing. "He has brought the blind by a way that he knew not, and led him in a path that he has not known." For the last two or three years there has been a process going on, a continual interchange of seasons of seriousness and then of forgetfulness, and then again of seriousness soon after. In this state I came here, and as you may well conceive there was little seriousness amid the bustle of coming away.

After leaving Scotland, however, there was an interval of seriousness during the three days we were at sea — our departure from Aberdeen, the sea, recollections of the past, all were calculated to lead one to reflect. But after I came to Holland I think I was led to pray in earnest. More I cannot tell, for I know it not. "Whereas I was blind, now I see." I was long troubled with the idea that I must have some deep sight of my sins before I could be converted, and though I cannot yet say that I have had anything of that deep special sight into the guiltiness of sin which many people appear to have, yet I trust, and at present I feel as if I could say, I am confident that as a sinner I have been led to cast myself on Christ.

What can I say now, my dear Parents, but call on you to praise the Lord with me? "Bless the Lord, O my soul, and all that is within me, bless His holy name. Bless the Lord, O my soul, and forget not all His benefits. Who forgives all your iniquities, who heals all your diseases; who redeems your life from destruction, who crowns you with loving-kindness and tender mercy." At present I am in a peaceful state. I cannot say that I have had any seasons of special joy, but I think that I enjoy a *true* confidence in God. Short, however, as my experience has been, I cannot say that it is always that way. Already I have felt my sins separating between me and my God, and then the miserable consequences, a sort of fear, and the wretched feeling of being held back in prayer by sin.

24th November. — In taking up my pen again, I have again to lament my inability to write on the great subject. Though I can say that my heart at present is warm, yet whenever I begin to write or speak, I fail. I sometimes think how glorious it will be when it shall be impossible to do anything but ascribe praise to Him who has loved us and washed us from our sins in His blood, and has made us kings and priests unto God. There certainly must be a great change in us before we shall be ready to do that. [2]

The following letter was written by Andrew to his parents six months later, just before his eighteenth birthday:

Tomorrow will close a year which is certainly the most eventful in my life, a year in which I have been made to experience most abundantly that God is good to the soul that seeks Him. And oh! what goodness it is when He Himself implants in us the desire of seeking while we are enemies. I rather think that when I last wrote I gave an account of what I believed was my conversion, and, God be thanked, I still believe that it was His work. Since the letter I cannot say that I have always had as much enjoyment as before it, but still there has been much joy in the Lord, though, alas! there has also been much sin. But through grace I have always been enabled to trust in Him who has begun the good work in me, and to believe that He will also perform what He has begun out of His free love before I was born. Oh! that I might receive grace to walk more holy before Him. [3]

Andrew again writes to his parents from Utrecht, expressing his desires to trust the Lord and his appreciation for his praying parents:

I am prepared for whatever shall be good, trusting that that gracious Father will guide us now, as He has so kindly led us up to now, and believing that He knows what is best for His Church in that part of the vineyard where I desire to labor. My desire is to place myself in His hands, and He can use me even though I do not have the advantage of an additional year's stay in Europe —

perhaps even better than if I had such an additional stock of human wisdom, which so often proves nothing else than an obstruction in God's way.

I say it is my wish to do this, for, alas! the general state of my mind is not so much a resting in faith in God's leadings, but a certain indifference and contentedness as to the future, resulting from my natural character. What a blessed thing it would be if we could commit ourselves and all our cares to Him in faith, in that active and living faith. I find that I so often mistake faith for a certain state of the mind which is content with the future, not of God's fatherly care, but of God's providence as something close to fate — an idea that I can't help it, and that there is no use in troubling about it. Oh! how different is the faith which arises from a soul really concerned in its own interests and in God's glory, the faith that sees and feels human aid insufficient and failing, and then flees to Him who is the strong refuge.

I am sure we have often been reaping the fruits of your believing prayers, while we were still unacquainted with true prayer, and I trust that we may still go on to experience what a blessing praying parents are. I must reproach myself, too, that I feel this so little, and that I so little seek in prayer those blessings for you, which we have so often received from you through this means. The Lord teach us to pray, and oh! although I do not pray for it as I ought, may He grant you a rich answer to the many prayers you have offered for us in an abundant blessing for your own souls. I am sure there are no prayers which parents offer, of which the answer is more gratifying to their own souls, than those which they see answered in the conversion of their children. May a gracious God, who has so far richly blessed the family in the conversion of the four oldest, unite us all in those ties which are closer than those of earthly relationship, and make us one in Christ. Remember us to all the family. [4]

Like Andrew Murray, your life may have been impacted by many godly influences. Your parents have prayed much for you. You have been exposed to the gospel of Jesus Christ. You have known the tug of the Spirit on your heart to open to Christ, but up to now, you have not responded.

The Lord Jesus wants to get your attention. In Revelation 3:19-20 He says, [19] "As many as I love, I rebuke and chasten. Therefore be zealous and repent. [20] Behold, I stand at the door and knock. If anyone hears My voice and opens the door, I will come in to him and dine with him, and he with Me." The word "behold" is spoken because the Lord seeks to secure our attention concerning our salvation. He wants us to consider that all the things that have impacted our lives positively and negatively are for one thing — to cause us to open the door of our heart and let Him in.

Andrew Murray reflected on his whole life, and by doing so, he stopped to *behold* that it was Christ standing at his door knocking. He then opened up to Him, and Christ came in and ushered him into a new life of enjoyment and spiritual feasting. This life is waiting for you now. The moment you open and say to the Lord, "Come in," He will immediately enter into your life and change you forever.

12 Hannah W. Smith

• A Discovery of God •

"It was a plan of
salvation that I could
understand...It was all
the work of Another
done for me."

(1832-1911)

*H*annah *Whitall Smith's book,* The Christian's
Secret of a Happy Life, *is a spiritual classic and
has helped countless numbers of Christians to understand the true nature of the Christian life. Hannah, along
with her husband, Robert Pearsall Smith, is also known
for founding the famous Keswick Convention for the
cultivation of the "higher Christian life."*

*Hannah's personal discovery of God came after a
process of searching that began with what she called
"the aching void in my heart." This aching void was
temporarily satisfied by the aid of a teacher named
Anna. Anna spoke to her of giving up all to the Savior,
but she did not show Hannah the way, except to admon-
ish her, "Let us struggle for a portion of His Spirit."*

Because of this kind of inner realization, Hannah was feeling deep desires for God but did not know how to find Him. Thus, she was plunged into a period which she called "morbid self-introspection." Her daily cry became "How do I feel?" not "What does God say?" She characterized her relationship with God at that time as being based on how she felt toward God, not on how God felt toward her.

After being in this state of introspection for a few years, Hannah was driven into skepticism for a period of two years. She then went through a season where she was "cold and dead again and full of pride!" Her idol was "the pride of human reason," and she confessed that she was in "a state of sad perplexity." At this point, when she was about to speak out her skepticism and doubts to others, an event took place that changed the whole course of her life. She tells about this event in her own words, revealing how she found Christ:

IT WAS IN THE YEAR 1858 and I was twenty-six years old. I had just lost a precious little daughter five years old, and my heart was aching with sorrow. I could not endure to think that my darling had gone out alone into a Godless universe; and yet, no matter on which side I turned, there seemed no ray of light.

It happened that just at this time the religious world was being greatly stirred by the inauguration of daily noonday meetings, held from twelve to one, in the business part of the city [Philadelphia], and crowded with businessmen. I had heard of these noonday meetings with a very languid interest, as I thought they were only another effort of a dying-out superstition to bolster up its cause. However, one day I happened to be near a place where one of these meetings was being held, and I thought I would go in and see what it was like. It was an impressive thing to see such crowds of busy men and women collected together at that hour in one of the busiest parts of the city, and I remember wondering vaguely what it could all be about.

Then suddenly something happened to me. What it was or how it came I had no idea, but somehow an inner eye seemed to be opened in my soul, and I seemed to see that, after all, God was a fact — the bottom fact of all facts — and that the only thing to do was to find out all about Him. It was not a pious feeling, such as I had been looking for, but it was a conviction — just such a conviction as comes to one when a mathematical problem is suddenly solved. One does not *feel* it is solved, but one knows it, and there can be no further question. I do not remember anything that was said. I do not even know that I heard anything. A tremendous revolution was going on within me that was of far profounder interest than anything the most eloquent preacher could have uttered. God was making Himself manifest as an actual existence, and my soul leaped up in an irresistible cry to know Him.

It was not that I felt myself to be a sinner needing salvation, or that I was troubled about my future destiny. It was not a personal question at all. It was simply and only that I had become aware of God, and that I felt I could not rest until I should know Him. I might be good or I might be bad; I might be going to Heaven or I might be going to hell — these things were outside the question. All I wanted was to become acquainted with the God of whom I had suddenly become aware.

How to set about it was the one absorbing question. I had no one I cared to ask, and it never occurred to me that prayer would help me. It seemed to me like the study of some new and wonderful branch of knowledge to which I must apply with all diligence, and I concluded that probably the Bible was the book I needed. "This book," I said to myself, "professes to teach us about God. I will see if it can teach me anything." I was going with my family to spend some weeks at the seashore, and I decided to take no books but the Bible, and to try and find out what it said about God. In my diary I wrote under the date of July 16, 1858 —

I have brought my Bible to Atlantic City this summer with a determination to find out what its plan of salvation is. My own plans have failed utterly, now I will try God's if possible....I am trying to believe Him simply as a little child. I have laid aside my preconceived notions of what He ought to do and say, and have come in simplicity to the Bible to see what He has done and said; and I *will* believe Him.

Someone had remarked once in my hearing that the book of Romans contained the clearest and fullest statements of Christian doctrine to be found in the Bible, and I set myself to read it. What I should have made out of it without any guidance I cannot say, but one day I mentioned to a lady, who was visiting us, how interested I was in trying to understand the teaching of the Book of Romans, but how difficult I found it. She said she had a little book which had explained it to her, and asked if she might give it to me. I accepted it eagerly, and found it most enlightening. It set forth the plan of salvation as described in the third, fourth and fifth chapters of Romans in a clear businesslike way that appealed to me strongly. It stated that mankind were all sinners, and all deserved punishment — that all had sinned and come short of the glory of God, and that there was none righteous, no not one; and it declared that therefore every mouth was stopped and all the world had become guilty before God (Rom. 3:1-19). It went on to show that there was no escape from this except through the righteousness of Christ, which was "unto all and upon all them that believe"; and that Christ was our propitiation, through whom we obtained the "remission of sins that are past" (Rom. 3:20-26). And then it pointed out that by this process all boasting on our part was shut out, and we were justified before God, not by anything we had done or could do, but by what our Divine Savior had done for us (Rom. 3:27-31). It declared that Christ was the substitute for sinners — that He had in their place borne the punishment they deserved, and that all we had to do in order to secure the full benefit of this substitution was simply to believe in it, and accept the forgiveness so purchased.

Of course this was a very legal and businesslike interpretation of these passages, and was not at all the interpretation I should give to them now; but I want to tell, as truthfully as I can, the way things impressed me then. The very crudeness and outwardness of the interpretation made it easy for my ignorance to grasp it, and it struck me at the time as a most sensible and satisfactory arrangement. It was a "plan of salvation" that I could understand. There was nothing mystical or mysterious about it — no straining after emotions, no looking out for experiences. It was all the work of Another done for me, and required nothing on my part but a simple common-sense understanding and belief.

Baldly stated, it was as follows. We were all sinners, and therefore all deserved punishment. But Christ had taken our sins upon Himself and had borne the punishment in our stead, and therefore an angry God was propitiated, and was willing to forgive us and let us go free. Nothing could be more plain and simple. Even a child could understand it. It was all outside of oneself, and there need be no searchings within or rakings up of one's inward feelings to make things right with God. Christ had made them right, and we had nothing to do but to accept it all as a free gift from Him. Moreover, a God who could arrange such a simple plan as this, was understandable and get-at-able, and I began to think it must be true.

This all sounds very outward and very crude; but, after all, crude as it seems, there was behind it the great bottom fact that God was, somehow or other, in Christ reconciling the world unto Himself; and it was this vital fact of the reconciliation between God and man that had laid hold of me. And I believe it is this fact, however it may be expressed, that is the one essential thing in the outset of every satisfactory religious life. The soul must know that all is right between itself and God before it can try, with any heart, to worship and serve Him.

I had discovered this vital fact, and the religious life had begun for me with eager and enthusiastic delight.

In my diary I find in 1858 the following entries:

RESTORATION OF BELIEF

August 20, 1858. Am I really coming to Christ? I ask myself this question with wonder and amazement. A month ago it seemed so utterly impossible. But I believe I am. It seems as if these truths in the New Testament have taken hold of my soul, and I cannot gainsay them. God only knows what the end will be.

August 21, 1858. Many passages of Scripture have been impressed on my mind in my reading, and, having made up my mind simply to believe and not to reason or question, I *do* find myself inevitably brought to Christ as my Redeemer. My watchword for the last few weeks has been "Thus says the Lord" as a conclusive argument in every case.

August 30, 1858. I am resting now simply on God's own record as the foundation of my hope. He says Jesus Christ is His well beloved Son, and I believe it. He says further that He gave His Son to be the propitiation for our sins, and I believe this also. He *is* my Savior, not only my helper; and in His finished work I rest. Even my hard heart of unbelief can no longer refrain from crying out, "Lord, I believe. Help Thou my unbelief."

September 13, 1858. My heart is filled with the exceeding preciousness of Christ. And I am lost in wonder at the realization of His infinite mercy to me, who am so utterly unworthy of the least favor from

His hands. How could He be so tender and so loving! I can write the words, "It is all of free grace," but they only feebly convey the deep sense I have of the infinite freeness of this grace. "While we were yet sinners Christ died for us." Could anything be more free than this? I have so long bewildered myself with trying to work out my own righteousness, and have found such weariness in it, that I feel as if I could never appreciate deeply enough the blessed rest there is for me in Christ. "He was made sin for us who knew no sin, that we might be made the righteousness of God in Him." No wonder the Apostle cried out from a full heart, "Thanks be unto God for His unspeakable gift!"

My diary is full of similar records, but these will suffice to tell of the wonderful discovery I had made. I want it to be clearly understood that it all came to me as a discovery, and in no sense as an attainment. I had been seeking after attainments in the past, but now I had lost all thought of any attainment of my own in the blaze of my discoveries of the salvation through Christ. It was no longer in the slightest degree a question of what I was or what I could do, but altogether a question of what God was and of what He had done. I seemed to have left myself, as myself, out of it entirely, and to care only to find out all I could about the work of Christ.

The thing that amazed me was how I could have lived so long in a world that contained the Bible, and never have found all this before. Why had nobody ever told me? How could people, who had found it out, have kept such a marvelous piece of good news to themselves? Certainly I could not keep it to myself, and I determined that no one whom I could reach should be left a day longer in ignorance, as far as I could help it. I began to buttonhole everybody, pulling them into corners and behind doors to tell them of the wonderful and delightful things I had discovered in the Bible about the salvation through the Lord Jesus Christ. It seemed to me the most magnificent piece of good news that any human being had ever had to tell, and I gloried in telling it.

So little however had I known of Christian ideas and Christian nomenclature, that I had not the least conception that what I had discovered made any difference in me personally, or that my belief in all this made me what they called a Christian. It only seemed to me that I had found out something delightful about God, which had filled me with happiness, and which I wanted everybody else to know. But that this discovery constituted what was called "conversion," or that I personally was different in any way from what I had been before, never entered my head.

One day, however, a "Plymouth Brother" friend, hearing me tell my story, exclaimed, "Thank God, Mrs. Smith, that you have at last become a Christian." So little did I understand him, that I promptly replied, "Oh, no, I am not a Christian at all. I have only found out a wonderful piece of good news that I never knew before." "But," he persisted, "that very discovery makes you a Christian, for the Bible says that whoever believes this good news has passed from death unto life, and is born of God. *You* have just said that you believe it and rejoice in it, so of course *you* have passed from death unto life and are born of God." I thought for a moment, and I saw the logic of what he said. There was no escaping it. And with a sort of gasp I said, "Why, so I must be. Of course I believe this good news, and therefore of course I must be born of God. Well, I *am* glad."

From that moment the matter was settled, and not a doubt as to my being a child of God and the possessor of eternal life has ever had the slightest power over me since. I rushed to my Bible to make myself sure there was no mistake, and I found it brimming over with this teaching. "He that believes *has*," "He that believes *is.*" There seemed to be nothing more to be said about it. Three passages especially struck me: 1 John 5:1, "Whoever believes that Jesus is the Christ is born of God"; and John 5:24, "Most assuredly, I say to you, he who hears My word and believes in Him who sent Me, has everlasting life, and shall not come into judgment, but has passed from death into life"; and above all, John 20:30, 31, "And truly Jesus did many other signs in the presence of His disciples, which are not written in this book; but these are written that you may believe that Jesus is the Christ, the Son of God, and that believing, you may have life through His name."

There seemed nothing more to be said. There were the things about Christ, written in the Bible, as clear as daylight, and I believed what was written with all my heart and soul, and therefore I could not doubt that I was one of those who had "life through His name." The question was settled without any further argument. It had nothing to do with how I felt, but only with what God had said. The logic seemed to me irresistible; and it not only convinced me then, but it has carried me triumphantly through every form of doubt as to my relations with God which has ever assailed me since. And I can recommend it as an infallible receipt to every doubter.

Of course at once, on having made this further discovery of the fact that I was a Christian, I began to add it to the story I had already been telling, always ending my recital with the words — "And now, if you believe all this, you are a Christian, for the Bible says that he that believes *is* born of God, and *has* eternal life."

I had got hold of that which is the necessary foundation of all religion, namely, reconciliation with God, and had had my first glimpse of Him as He is revealed in the face of Jesus Christ. All my fear of Him had vanished. He loved me, He forgave me, He was on my side, and all was right between us. I had learned moreover that it was from the life and words of Christ that my knowledge of God was to come, and not, as I had always thought, from my own inward feelings; and my relief was inexpressible.

I can see now, in looking back, that in many respects I had only touched the surface of the spiritual realities hidden under the doctrines I had so eagerly embraced. I was as yet only in the beginning of things. But it was a beginning in the right direction, and was the introduction to the "life more abundant" which, as my story will show, was to come later. Meanwhile I had got my first glimpse of the unselfishness of God. As yet it was only a glimpse, but it was enough to make me radiantly happy. [1]

◆

As Hannah Whitall Smith found, salvation is a discovery and not an attainment. If salvation were an attainment, then we would be thrown back on our record, our history, our performance, our own righteousness, our states of mind, our feelings, and our own ability to measure up to a standard. Salvation based on man's attainment is completely discounted by the following verses:

"Not by works of righteousness which we have done, but according to His mercy He saved us" (Titus 3:5).

[8] "For by grace you have been saved through faith, and that not of yourselves; it is the gift of God, [9] not of works, lest anyone should boast" (Eph. 2:8-9).

"And if by grace, then it is no longer of works; otherwise grace is no longer grace" (Rom. 11:6).

Such verses disarm us from seeking to attain salvation based on anything we can do. Salvation is totally a discovery — a revelation — a seeing of what Christ has done for us! It is all the work of Another, done for us even when we were dead and enemies of God. Romans 5:10 declares, "For if when we were enemies we were reconciled to God through the death of His Son, much more, having been reconciled, we shall be saved in His life." Thus, to be reconciled to God is altogether the *work* of Another, and to be saved is altogether a matter of the *life* of Another. It is all in the realm of discovery, not attainment.

You can make this wonderful discovery by simply stopping yourself from establishing your own righteousness, and submitting yourself to the righteousness of God. The righteousness of God is Christ! Period! That is all. You need do nothing else. You need look no further. Romans 10:4 tells us, "For Christ is the end of the law for righteousness to everyone who believes." Christ is now waiting to come into your heart. He is waiting for you to discover Him. Let Romans 10:8-9 lead you to this awesome discovery of Christ:

> [8] "The word is near you, in your mouth and in your heart (that is, the word of faith which we preach): [9] that if you confess with your mouth the Lord Jesus and believe in your heart that God has raised Him from the dead, you will be saved."

13 J. Hudson Taylor

• Ignorance of the Gospel •

"If the whole work was
finished and the whole
debt paid, what is there
left for me to do?"

(1832-1905)

*A*lthough J. Hudson Taylor was raised in a Christian
home, he remained ignorant of what it really meant
to become a Christian. He even tried to "make" himself
a Christian, but after failing in his attempts, he became
skeptical of the things of God. However, at the age of
seventeen, Taylor read a gospel tract that opened his
eyes to see the finished work of Christ. That day he found
Christ. He was soon burdened for the gospel to reach
China, which was virtually a closed empire at that time.
After years of preparation, he left England, arriving in
Shanghai in 1854.

   Desiring to live as much as possible like the people
he was so burdened to reach, Taylor became the first
missionary to adopt Chinese dress. His ambition was
"to evangelize all China, to preach Christ to all its

peoples by any and all means that come to hand." In this endeavor he lived without human guarantee of material support, believing that the God who had called him would supply all his needs.

For over fifty years God proved His faithfulness to Taylor and largely granted his heart's desire to reach the whole of China. By the time of his death in 1905, the China Inland Mission, formed by him some forty years earlier, was the most prevailing Christian work in China. The following, from Taylor's autobiography, is an account of his rebirth experience:

FOR MYSELF, and for the work that I have been permitted to do for God, I owe an unspeakable debt of gratitude to my beloved and honored parents, who have passed away and entered into rest, but the influence of whose lives will never pass away.

Many years ago, probably about 1830, the heart of my dear father, then himself an earnest and successful evangelist at home, was deeply stirred as to the spiritual state of China by reading several books, and especially an account of the travels of Captain Basil Hall. His circumstances were such as to preclude the hope of his ever going to China for personal service, but he was led to pray that if God should give him a son, he might be called and privileged to labor in the vast, needy empire which was then apparently so sealed against the truth. I was not aware of this desire or prayer myself until my return to England, more than seven years after I had sailed for China; but it was very interesting then to know how prayer offered before my birth had been answered in this matter.

All thought of my becoming a missionary was abandoned for many years by my dear parents on account of the feebleness of my health. When the time came, however, God gave increased health, and my life has been spared, and strength has been given for not a little toilsome service, both in the mission field and at home, while many stronger men and women have succumbed.

I had many opportunities in early years of learning the value of prayer and of the Word of God; for it was the delight of my dear parents to point out that if there were any such Being as God, to trust Him, to obey Him, and to be fully given up to His service must, of necessity, be the best and wisest course both for myself and others. But in spite of these helpful examples and precepts, my heart was unchanged. Often I had tried to make myself a Christian; and failing of course in such efforts, I began at last to think that for some reason or other I could not be saved, and that the best I could do was to take my fill of this world, as there was no hope for me beyond the grave.

While in this state of mind, I came in contact with persons holding skeptical and infidel views, and accepted their teaching, only too thankful for some hope of escape from the doom which, if my parents were right and the Bible true, awaited the impenitent. It may seem strange to say it, but I have often felt thankful for the experience of this time of skepticism. The inconsistencies of Christian people, who, while professing to believe their Bibles, were yet content to live just as they would if there were no such Book, had been one of the strongest arguments of my skeptical companions. I frequently felt at that time and said, that if I pretended to believe the Bible, I would at any rate attempt to live by it, putting it fairly to the test; and if it failed to prove true and reliable, I would throw it overboard altogether. These views I retained when the Lord was pleased to bring me to Himself, and I think I may say that since then I *have* put God's Word to the test. Certainly it has never failed me. I have never had reason to regret the confidence I have placed in its promises or to deplore following the guidance I have found in its directions.

Let me tell you how God answered the prayers of my dear mother and of my beloved sister, now Mrs. Broomhall, for my conversion. On a day which I shall never forget, when I was about seventeen years of age, my dear mother was absent from home and I had a holiday. In the afternoon I looked through my father's library to find some book with which to while away the unoccupied hours. Nothing attracting me, I turned over a little basket of pamphlets, and selected from among them a gospel tract which looked interesting, saying to myself, "There will be a story at the beginning, and a sermon or moral at the close: I will take the former and leave the latter for those who like it."

I sat down to read the little book in an utterly unconcerned state of mind, believing indeed at the time that if there were any salvation it was not for me, and with a distinct intention to put away the tract as soon as it should seem dull. I may say that it was not uncommon in those days to call conversion "becoming serious." And judging by the faces of some of its professors, it appeared to be a very serious matter indeed. Would it not be well if the people of God had always telltale faces, evincing the blessings and gladness of salvation so clearly that unconverted people might have to call conversion "becoming joyful" instead of "becoming serious"?

Little did I know at the time what was going on in the heart of my dear mother, seventy or eighty miles away. She rose from the dinner table that afternoon with an intense yearning for the conversion of her boy, and feeling that — absent from home, and having more leisure than she could otherwise secure — a special opportunity was afforded her of pleading with God on my behalf. She went to her room and turned the key in the door, resolved not to leave that spot until her prayers were answered. Hour after hour did that dear mother plead for me, until at length she could pray no longer, but was constrained to praise God for that which His Spirit taught her had already been accomplished — the conversion of her only son.

I in the meantime had been led in the way I have mentioned to take up this little tract, and while reading it was struck with the sentence, "The finished work of Christ." The thought passed through my mind, "Why does the author use this expression? Why not say the atoning or propitiatory work of Christ?" Immediately the words "It is finished" suggested themselves to my mind. What was finished? And I at once replied, "A full and perfect atonement and satisfaction for sin: the debt was paid by the Substitute; Christ died for our sins, and not for ours only, but also for the sins of the whole world." Then came the thought, "If the whole work was finished and the whole debt paid, what is there left for me to do?" And with this dawned the joyful conviction, as light was flashed into my soul by the Holy Spirit, that there was nothing in the world to be done but to fall down on one's knees, and accepting this Savior and His salvation, to praise Him forevermore. Thus while my dear mother was praising God on her knees in her chamber, I was praising Him in the old warehouse to which I had gone alone to read this little book at my leisure.

Several days elapsed before I ventured to make my beloved sister the confidante of my joy, and then only after she had promised not to tell anyone of my soul secret. When our dear mother came home two weeks later, I was the first to meet her at the door, and to tell her I had such glad news to give. I can almost feel that dear mother's arms around my neck, as she pressed me to her bosom and said, "I know, my boy; I have been rejoicing for two weeks in the glad tidings you have to tell me." "Why," I asked in surprise, "has Amelia broken her promise? She said she would tell no one." My dear mother assured me that it was not from any human source that she had learned the tidings, and went on to tell the little incident mentioned above. You will agree with me that it would be strange indeed if I were not a believer in the power of prayer.

Nor was that all. Some little time after, I picked up a pocketbook exactly like one of my own, and thinking that it was mine, opened it. The lines that caught my eye were an entry in the little diary, which belonged to my sister, to the effect that she would give herself daily to prayer until God should answer in the conversion of her brother. Exactly one month later the Lord was pleased to turn me from darkness to light.

Brought up in such a circle and saved under such circumstances, it was perhaps natural that from the beginning of my Christian life I was led to feel that the promises were very real, and that prayer was a sober matter-of-fact transacting business with God, whether on one's own behalf or on behalf of those for whom one sought His blessing. [1]

---◆---

Hudson Taylor's ignorance of the gospel message was erased when he grasped the meaning of "the finished work of Christ." Not knowing this crucial fact of Christ's finished work is a common reason why many people never find Christ. Have you ever come face to face with the question, What does the finished work of Christ mean to me? Do I realize *why* Christ died on the cross? Like Hudson Taylor's experience, our whole life can be changed by being enlightened about the cross.

You must understand that when Jesus said from the cross, "It is finished!" everything that God requires from you was taken care of, and everything that you need to be in order to be accepted by God was accomplished (John 19:30). This is because Christ has been appointed by God to be our Substitute. Isaiah 53:4-6 makes this clear: [4] "Surely He has borne our griefs and carried our sorrows; yet we esteemed Him stricken, smitten by God, and afflicted. [5] But He was wounded for our transgressions, He was bruised for our iniquities; the chastisement for our peace was upon Him, and by His stripes we are healed. [6] All we like sheep have gone astray; we have turned, every one, to his own way; and the LORD has laid on Him the iniquity of us all." Christ is our Substitute!

When you see that God "made Him who knew no sin to be sin for us, that we might become the righteousness of God in Him" (2 Cor. 5:21), there is only one question to ask — "What is there left for me to do?"

Like Taylor, when you see that Christ's work on the cross is a finished work, you also see that there is absolutely nothing to do but to accept this Savior and His salvation, and then to praise Him forever. Tell the Lord now from your heart that you rest in His finished work accomplished on the cross. Thank Him that your sins are forgiven! Your peace with God is made! Christ now lives in you! Just enjoy this fact — "For by grace you have been saved through faith, *and that not of yourselves; it is the gift of God, not of works,* lest anyone should boast. For we are His workmanship, created in Christ Jesus" (Eph. 2:8-10).

14 Charles Spurgeon

• A Seeking Heart •

"Look unto Me!…I had
been waiting to do fifty
things, but when I heard
that word, 'Look!' what
a charming word it
seemed to me!"

(1834-1892)

*C*harles Spurgeon was raised in a godly home in
England. Both his father and grandfather were
ministers of the gospel. At the age of ten, he began to
seek God regarding his own salvation. After a period of
about five years, he happened to attend a Primitive
Methodist meeting in which the passage, "Look unto
Me, and be ye saved," was being preached. That day
Spurgeon found Christ.

Soon Spurgeon himself began to preach. He was so
effective that by the age of nineteen this "boy-preacher"
was attracting large crowds in London to hear the gospel
of Christ. He continued preaching in that city, primarily
at the Metropolitan Tabernacle, for thirty-eight years
until his death in 1892. The following, taken from his

book, Conversion: the Great Change, *gives an account of the day he found Christ.*

I SOMETIMES THINK I might have been in darkness and despair until now had it not been for the goodness of God in sending a snowstorm one Sunday morning while I was going to a certain place of worship. When I could go no further, I turned down a side street, and came to a little Primitive Methodist Chapel. In that chapel there may have been a dozen or fifteen people. I had heard of the Primitive Methodists, how they sang so loudly that they made people's heads ache; but that did not matter to me. I wanted to know how I might be saved, and if they could tell me that, I did not care how much they made my head ache. The minister did not come that morning; he was snowed up, I suppose. At last, a very thin-looking man, a shoemaker, or tailor, or something of that sort, went up into the pulpit to preach. Now, it is well that preachers should be instructed; but this man was really stupid. He was obliged to stick to his text, for the simple reason that he had little else to say. The text was —

> "LOOK UNTO ME, AND BE YE SAVED,
> ALL THE ENDS OF THE EARTH!"

He did not even pronounce the words rightly, but that did not matter. There was, I thought, a glimpse of hope for me in that text. The preacher began thus: "My dear friends, this is a very simple text indeed. It says, 'Look.' Now lookin' don't take a deal of pains. It ain't liftin' your foot or your finger; it is just, 'Look.' Well, a man needn't go to college to learn to look. You may be the biggest fool, and yet you can look. A man needn't be worth a thousand a year to be able to look. Anyone can look; even a child can look. But then the text says, 'Look unto *Me*.' Ay!" said he, in broad Essex, "many on ye are lookin' to yourselves, but it's no use lookin' there. You'll never find any comfort in yourselves. Some look to God the Father. No, look to Him by-and-by. Jesus Christ says, 'Look unto *Me*.' Some on ye say, 'We must wait for the Spirit's workin'.' You have no business with that just now. Look to *Christ*. The text says, 'Look unto *Me*.' "

Then the good man followed up his text in this way: "Look unto Me; I am sweatin' great drops of blood. Look unto Me; I am hangin' on the cross. Look unto Me; I am dead and buried. Look unto Me; I rise again. Look unto Me; I ascend to heaven. Look unto Me; I am sittin' at the Father's right hand. O poor sinner, look unto Me! look unto Me!"

When he had gone to about that length, and managed to spin out ten minutes or so, he was at the end of his tether. Then he looked at me under the gallery, and I daresay, with so few present, he knew me to be a stranger. Just fixing his eyes on me, as if he knew all my heart, he said, "Young man, you look very miserable." Well, I did; but I had not been accustomed to have remarks made from the pulpit on my personal appearance before. However, it was a good blow, struck right home. He continued, "and you always will be miserable — miserable in life, and miserable in death — if you don't obey my text; but if you obey now, this moment, you will be saved." Then, lifting up his hands, he shouted, as only a Primitive Methodist could do, "Young man, look to Jesus Christ. Look! Look! Look! You have nothin' to do but to look and live." I saw at once the way of salvation.

I know not what else he said — I did not take much notice of it — I was so possessed with that one thought. Like as when the brazen serpent was lifted up, the people only looked and were healed, so it was with me. I had been waiting to do fifty things, but when I heard that word, "Look!" what a charming word it seemed to me! Oh! I looked until I could almost have looked my eyes away. There and then the cloud was gone, the darkness had rolled away, and that moment I saw the sun; and I could have risen that instant and sung with the most enthusiastic of them, of the precious blood of Christ, and the simple faith which looks alone to Him. Oh, that somebody had told me this before, "Trust Christ and you shall be saved." Yet it was, no doubt, all wisely ordered, and now I can say —

"E'er since by faith I saw the stream
Thy flowing wounds supply,
Redeeming love has been my theme,
and shall be till I die."

I do from my soul confess that I never was satisfied till I came to Christ; when I was yet a child, I had far more wretchedness than ever I have now; I will even add, more weariness, more care, more heartache than I know at this day. I may be singular in this confession, but I make it, and know it to be the truth. Since that dear hour when my soul cast itself on Jesus, I have found solid joy and peace; but before that, all those supposed gaieties of early youth, all the imagined ease and joy of boyhood, were but vanity and vexation of spirit to me. That happy day, when I found the Savior and learned to cling to His dear feet, was a day never to be forgotten by me.

An obscure child, unknown, unheard of, I listened to the Word of God; and that precious text led me to the cross of Christ. I can testify that the joy of that day was utterly indescribable. I could have leaped, I could have danced; there was no expression, however fanatical, which would have been out of keeping with the joy of my spirit at that hour. Many days of Christian experience have passed since then, but there has never been one which has had the full exhilaration, the sparkling delight which that first day had. I thought I could have sprung from the seat on which I sat, and have called out with the wildest of those Methodist brethren who were present, "I am forgiven! I am forgiven! A monument of grace! A sinner saved by blood!" My spirit saw its chains broken to pieces. I felt that I was an emancipated soul, an heir of heaven, a forgiven one, accepted in Christ Jesus, plucked out of the miry clay and out of the horrible pit, with my feet set upon a rock, and my goings established. I thought I could dance all the way home. I could understand what John Bunyan meant, when he declared he wanted to tell the crows on the ploughed land all about his conversion. He was too full to hold. He felt he must tell somebody.

It is not everyone who can remember the very day and hour of his deliverance; but, as Richard Knill said, "At such a time of the day, clang went every harp in heaven, for Richard Knill was born again," it was e'en so with me. The clock of mercy struck in heaven the hour and moment of my emancipation, for the time had come. Between half-past ten o'clock, when I entered that chapel, and half-past twelve o'clock, when I was back again at home, what a change had taken place in me! I had passed from darkness into marvelous light, from death to life. Simply by looking to Jesus, I had been delivered from despair, and I was brought into such a joyous state of mind that, when they saw me at home, they said to me, "Something wonderful has happened to you"; and I was eager to tell them all about it. Oh! there was joy in the household that day, when all heard that the eldest son had found the Savior and knew himself to be forgiven — bliss compared with which all earth's joys are less than nothing and vanity.

Yes, I had looked to Jesus as I was, and found in Him my Savior. Thus had the eternal purpose of Jehovah decreed it; and, as the moment before, there was none more wretched than I was, so, within that second, there was none more joyous. It took no longer time than does the lightning flash; it was done, and never has it been undone. I looked, and lived, and leaped in joyful liberty as I beheld my sin punished upon the great Substitute and put away forever. I looked unto Him, as He bled upon that tree; His eyes darted a glance of love unutterable into my spirit, and in a moment, I was saved. Looking unto Him, the bruises that my soul had suffered were healed, the gaping wounds were cured, the broken bones rejoiced, the rags that had covered me were all removed, and my spirit was white as the spotless snows of the far-off North. I had melody within my spirit, for I was saved, washed, cleansed, forgiven, through Him that did hang upon the tree. [1]

---◆---

Like Charles Spurgeon, when a person has a seeking heart and wants to know how to be saved, any instrument or way God wants to use to point him to Christ is acceptable. Some people want to find Christ on their own terms and in their own way, but if your heart is seeking, you will find Christ on whatever terms and in whatever way God chooses to use. Romans 8:28 says, "And we know that *all* things work together for good to those who love God, to those who are the called according to His purpose." Right now all things in your life are working together for "good," and that good, according to God's Word, is that you would receive Jesus Christ into your life.

Jesus said, "For what is a man profited if he gains the whole world, and loses his own soul?" (Matt. 16:26). What are you seeking? Nothing will satisfy you ultimately. Even if you attained the highest human goal or could actually own the whole world, still, apart from Christ, you would be left with an emptiness inside. Your seeking needs to be focused, like Spurgeon's, to look to Christ and be saved. Isaiah 45:22 declares, "Look unto Me, and be ye saved, all the ends of the earth: for I am God, and there is none else."

You can turn your seeking of Christ into finding Him by following Paul's specific answer to the Philippian jailor's question, "Sirs, what must I do to be saved?" Paul said, "Believe on the Lord Jesus Christ, and you will be saved" (Acts 16:30-31). This is how to find Christ — *believe on Him,* not by merely giving mental assent, but by making contact with Him in prayer, confessing Him as Lord. It works! Romans 10:11-12 says, [11] "Whoever believes on Him will not be put to shame. [12] For there is no distinction between Jew and Greek, for the same Lord over all is rich to *all who call upon Him*."

15 A. B. Simpson

• A Desperate Situation •

"My eyes fell upon a sentence which opened for me the gates of life eternal."

(1843-1919)

The spiritual influence of Albert Benjamin Simpson has not only touched the movement he founded, The Christian and Missionary Alliance, *but it has also affected seeking Christians from all evangelical persuasions. Simpson's early roots go back to a godly family. Both his father and mother were deeply devoted to the Lord. They lived their daily life according to the strictest principles of the Puritans. Indeed, family worship was often the occasion for reading the following classic Puritan writings: Thomas Boston's* Human Nature in Its Fourfold State, *Richard Baxter's* The Saints' Everlasting Rest, *and Philip Doddridge's* The Rise and Progress of Religion in the Soul.

Immediately following his conversion experience, Simpson wholly surrendered himself to the Lord. His surrender was based upon the prayer of surrender from Doddridge's book, part of which said, "The surrender will also be as entire as it is cheerful and immediate. All you are, and all you have, and all you can do, your time, your possessions, your influence over others, will be devoted to Him, that for the future it may be employed entirely for Him, and to His glory."

Yet, just before he found Christ, Simpson passed through a series of crises. One of these was a physical and nervous breakdown due to the pressures of study and domestic responsibilities. The doctor informed him that he was in "the greatest danger." In his testimony, Simpson describes the "dreadful nervousness" he passed through. It was a desperate situation, and to add to it all, he knew that he was without Christ.

During this critical time, Simpson picked up Walter Marshall's classic work, The Gospel Mystery of Sanctification. As he read, his eyes fell upon one sentence that changed the course of his whole life. Here Simpson tells in his own words how he came to this point:

MY CHILDHOOD AND YOUTH were strangely sheltered and guarded by divine providence. I recall with sacred awe many times when my life was almost miraculously preserved. On one occasion, while climbing up on the scaffolding of a building in course of erection, I stepped upon a loose board which tipped over and plunged me into space. Instinctively throwing out my hands, I caught a piece of timber, one of the flooring joists, and desperately held on, crying for assistance. When exhausted and about to fall, a workman caught me just in time. The fall would certainly have killed me or maimed me for life.

At another time I was thrown headlong over my horse's head as he stumbled and fell under me. When I came back to consciousness, I found him bending over me with his nose touching my face, almost as if he wanted to speak to me and encourage me. At another time I was kicked into unconsciousness by a dangerous horse, and still remember the awful struggle to recover my breath as I thought myself dying.

Once I had a remarkable escape from drowning. I had gone with one of my schoolmates in the high school to gather wild grapes on the banks of the river. After a while my companion tempted me to go in swimming, an art about which I knew nothing. In a few moments I got beyond my depth, and with an agony I shall always remember, I found myself choking under the surface. In that moment the whole of my life came before me as if in a vision, and I can well understand the stories told by drowning persons of the photograph that seems to come to their minds in the last moment of consciousness. I remember seeing, as clearly as if I had read it from the printed page, the notice in the local newspaper telling of my drowning and the grief and sorrow of my friends. Somehow God mercifully saved me. My companion was too frightened to help me, but his shouts attracted some men in a little boat a short distance away, and they pulled me out just as I was sinking for the last time, and laid me on the river bank. As I came back to consciousness a while afterwards, it seemed to me that years had passed since I was last on earth. I am sure that experience greatly deepened my spiritual earnestness.

But, like other boys, I often passed from the sublime to the ridiculous as this little incident will show. It was my good fortune to secure as a first prize in the high school an extremely handsome book which my chum, who had failed in the examination, had set his heart upon getting. He finally succeeded in tempting me by an old violin, with which he used to practice on my responsive heart, until at last I was persuaded to exchange my splendid prize for his old fiddle. The following summer I took it home and made night hideous and myself a general nuisance. I had never really succeeded in playing anything worthwhile, but there must have been somewhere in my nature a latent vein of music, and still to me the strains of the violin have a subtle inspirational power with which nothing else in music can be compared.

My first definite religious crisis came at about the age of fourteen. Prior to this I had for a good while been planning to study for the ministry. I am afraid that this came to me in the first instance rather as a conviction of duty than a spontaneous Christian impulse. There grew up in my young heart a great conflict about my future life; naturally I rebelled against the ministry because of the restraints which it would put upon many pleasures. One irresistible desire was to have a gun and to shoot and hunt; and I reasoned that if I were a minister, it would never do for me to indulge in such pastimes.

I was cured of this in a somewhat tragic way. I had saved up a little money, earned through special jobs and carefully laid aside, and one day I stole off to the town and invested it in a shot gun. For a few days I had the time of my life. I used to steal out to the woods with my forbidden idol and then with my sister's help smuggle it back to the attic. One day, however, my mother found it, and there was a never-to-be-forgotten scene. Her own brother had lost his life through the accidental discharge of a gun, and I knew and should have remembered that such things were prohibited in our family. It was a day of judgment for me; and when that wicked weapon was brought from its hiding place, I stood crushed and confounded as I was sentenced to the deep humiliation of returning it to the man from whom I bought it, losing not only my gun but my money too.

That tragedy settled the question of the ministry. I soon after decided to give up all side issues and prepare myself if I could only find a way to preach the Gospel.

But as yet the matter had not even been introduced in the family. One day, however, my father in his quiet, grave way, with my mother sitting by, called my elder brother and myself into his presence and began to explain that the former had long been destined to the ministry and that the time had now come when he should begin his studies and prepare to go to college. I should say that at this time we both had an excellent common school education. My father added that he had a little money, rescued from the wrecked business of many years before, now slowly coming in, which would be sufficient to give an education to one but not both of his boys. He quietly concluded that it would be my duty to stay at home on the farm while my brother went to college. I can still feel the lump that rose in my throat as I stammered out my acquiescence. Then I ventured with broken words and stammering tongue to plead that they would consent to my getting an education if I could work it out without asking anything from them but their approval and blessing. I had a little scheme of my own to teach school and earn the money for my education. But even this I did not dare to divulge, for I was but a lad of less than fourteen. I remember the quiet trembling tones with which my father received my request and said, "God bless you, my boy."

So the struggle began, and I shall never cease to thank God that it was a hard one. Someone has said, "Many people succeed because success is thrust upon them," but the most successful lives are those that began without a penny. Nothing under God has ever been a greater blessing to me than the hard places that began with me more than half a century ago, and have not yet ended.

For the first few months my brother and I took lessons in Latin, Greek and higher mathematics from a retired minister and then from our kind pastor, who was a good scholar and ready to help us in our purpose. Later I pursued my studies in Chatham High School, but the strain was too great, and I went back to my father's house a physical wreck. Then came a fearful crash in which it seemed to me the very heavens were falling. After retiring one night suddenly a star appeared to blaze before my eyes; and as I gazed, my nerves gave way. I sprang from my bed trembling and almost fainting with a sense of impending death, and then fell into a congestive chill of great violence that lasted all night and almost took my life. A physician told me that I must not look at a book for a whole year for my nervous system had collapsed, and I was in the greatest danger. There followed a period of mental and physical agony which no language can describe. I was possessed with the idea that at a certain hour I was to die; and every day as that hour drew near, I became prostrated with dreadful nervousness, watching in agonized suspense till the hour passed, and wondering that I was still alive.

One day the situation became so acute that nothing could stop it. Terrified and sinking, I called my father to my bedside and besought him to pray for me, for I felt I was dying. Worst of all I had no personal hope in Christ. My whole religious training had left me without any conception of the sweet and simple Gospel of Jesus Christ. The God I knew was a being of great severity, and my theology provided in some mysterious way for a wonderful change called the new birth or regeneration, which only God could give to the soul. How I longed and waited for that change to come, but it had not yet arrived. Oh, how my father prayed for me that day, and how I cried in utter despair for God to spare me just long enough to be saved!

After that dreadful sense of sinking, at last a little rest came, and the crisis was over for another day. I looked at the clock, and the hour had passed. I believed that God was going to spare me just one day more, and that I must strive and pray for salvation that whole day as a doomed man. How I prayed and besought others to pray, and almost feared to go to sleep that night lest I should lose a moment from my search for God and eternal life; but the day passed, and I was not saved. It now seems strange that there was no voice there to tell me the simple way of believing in the promise and accepting the salvation fully provided and freely offered. How often since then it has been my delight to tell poor sinners that —

"We do not need at Mercy's gate
To knock and weep, and watch and wait;
For Mercy's gifts are offered free,
And she has waited long for thee."

After that, as day after day passed, I rallied a little, and my life seemed to hang upon a thread, for I had the hope that God would spare me long enough to find salvation if I only continued to seek it with all my heart. Then one day, in the library of my old minister and teacher, I stumbled upon an old musty volume called *Marshall's Gospel Mystery of Sanctification*. As I turned the pages, my eyes fell upon a sentence which opened for me the gates of life eternal. It is this in substance: "The first good work you will ever perform is to believe on the Lord Jesus Christ. Until you do this, all your works, prayers, tears, and good resolutions are vain. To believe on the Lord Jesus is just to believe that He saves you according to His Word, that He receives and saves you here and now, for He has said — 'Him that comes to Me I will in no wise cast out.' The moment you do this, you will pass into eternal life, you will be justified from all your sins, and receive a new heart and all the gracious operations of the Holy Spirit."

To my poor bewildered soul this was like the light from heaven that fell upon Saul of Tarsus on his way to Damascus. I immediately fell upon my knees, and look-

ing up to the Lord, I said, "Lord Jesus, You have said —
Him that comes to Me I will in no wise cast out. You
know how long and earnestly I have tried to come, but I
did not know how. Now I come the best I can, and I dare
to believe that You do receive me and save me, and that
I am now Your child, forgiven and saved simply because
I have taken You at Your word. Abba Father, You are
mine, and I am Yours."

It is needless to say that I had a fight of faith with the
great Adversary before I was able to get out all these
words and dared to make this confession of my faith; but
I had no sooner made it and set my seal to it than there
came to my heart that divine assurance that always
comes to the believing soul, for "He who believes has the
witness in himself." I had been seeking the witness
without believing, but from the moment that I dared to
believe the Word, I had the assurance that —

> "The Spirit answers to the blood
> And tells me I am born of God." [1]

Like A. B. Simpson, you may find yourself in a
desperate situation, whatever it may be. Perhaps you
have been brought face to face with the realities of life
and even death itself — yet you have still not received

Christ into your life. At this juncture, you need to see that God works in desperate situations. In fact, God comes to us in these times.

It was the apostle Paul who desperately cried out in his personal state of defeat and failure, "O wretched man that I am! Who will deliver me from the body of this death?" (Rom. 7:24). The answer came instantly out of his own mouth, "I thank God *through* Jesus Christ." Immediately, he was delivered out of his despair into the rest and peace of knowing that Jesus Christ is God's unique answer for desperate souls. Now everything is handled and processed *through* Jesus Christ. Paul sums it up by saying, "It is no longer I who live, but Christ lives in me" (Gal. 2:20). Just as Paul and A. B. Simpson did, let Christ come in now, and then let Him do everything *in* you and *for* you forever!

16 Watchman Nee

· A Successful Life ·

"As I made my first
prayer I knew joy and
peace such as I had never
known before…Oh Lord,
You have indeed been
gracious to me."

(1903-1972)

Watchman Nee was a native of a province in Southern China. As a young man he proved himself to be a very intelligent and promising individual. He was consistently the top student in his classes, achieving an excellent academic record. He, of course, had many youthful dreams and plans for a successful career. Yet in 1920 at the age of seventeen, he came under the hearing of the gospel and, after some inward struggle, received Christ as his Savior and Lord.

The ministry of Watchman Nee has been one of the most significant and spiritual to emerge during this century. His labors had a profound effect upon the spreading of the gospel and the establishing of hundreds of local churches throughout Asia. Also, his many books

*and spoken messages have become a rich supply to
believers throughout the world.*

*Because of his faith, Nee was imprisoned in 1952
and remained so for the last twenty years of his life. His
last letters from prison revealed his faithfulness to the
Lord all the way to the end. Below is a brief testimony of
his salvation experience and the months immediately
following:*

M Y BIRTH was an answer to prayer. My mother
was fearful that she would follow her sister-in-
law in bearing six daughters, since, according to Chinese
custom, boys were preferable to girls. She had already
borne two daughters, and although she probably did not
fully understand the implications of prayer, she spoke to
the Lord and said, "If I should bear a son, I will present
him to You." The Lord heard her prayer, and I was born.
My father later told me that before my birth my mother
had promised to present me to the Lord.

For most people, the prominent feature of their being
saved is the act of being delivered from sin. However, for
me the question was whether I should accept Jesus and
become both His follower and His servant. I was frightened that if I became a Christian, then I would be called
upon to serve Christ, and that would be too costly.
Eventually the conflict was resolved as I realized that my
salvation must have two aspects. I decided to accept

Christ as my Savior and to serve Him as my Lord. The year was 1920, when I was seventeen years of age.

On the evening of 29th April, 1920, I was alone in my room, struggling to decide whether or not to believe in the Lord. At first I was reluctant, but as I tried to pray I saw the magnitude of my sins and the reality and efficacy of Jesus as the Savior. As I visualized the Lord's hands stretched out on the cross, they seemed to be welcoming me and the Lord was saying, "I am waiting here to receive you." Realizing the effectiveness of Christ's blood in cleansing my sins, and being overwhelmed by such love, I accepted Him there. Previously I had laughed at people who had accepted Jesus, but that evening the experience became real for me and I wept and confessed my sins, seeking the Lord's forgiveness. As I made my first prayer I knew joy and peace such as I had never known before. Light seemed to flood the room and I said to the Lord, "Oh Lord, You have indeed been gracious to me."

In the audience today there are at least three former schoolmates of mine, among whom Brother Kwang Hsi Weigh can bear testimony both to my bad behavior and excellent academic record at school. On the one hand I frequently broke the school rules, while on the other hand my God-given intelligence enabled me to come first in every examination. My essays were often put up for exhibition on the bulletin board. I trusted my judgment implicitly and had many youthful dreams and plans for my career. If I worked hard enough I believed that I could attain any level that I wished.

Following my being saved there were many changes, and all the planning of over ten years became meaningless, and my cherished ambitions were discarded. From that day, with the undoubted assurance of God's calling, I knew what my life's career was to be. I understood that the Lord had brought me to Himself both for my own salvation and for His glory. He had called me to serve Him and be His fellow-worker. Formerly I had despised preachers and preaching because in those days most preachers were the employees of European or American missionaries, having to be servile to them, and earning merely eight or nine silver dollars each month. I had never imagined for a moment that I would become a preacher, a profession which I regarded as trifling and base.

After my being saved, while others brought novels to read in class, I brought a Bible to study. Later on I left school to enter the Bible Institute established in Shanghai by Sister Dora Yu. Before very long she politely expelled me from the institute with the explanation that it was inconvenient for me to stay any longer. Because of my gourmet appetite, dilettante dress and tardy arising in the mornings, Sister Yu thought fit to send me home. My desire to serve the Lord had been dealt a serious blow. Although I thought my life had been transformed, in fact there remained many more things to be changed. Realizing that I was not yet ready for God's service, I decided to return to school. My schoolmates recognized that some things had altered but that much of my old temperament had remained. Therefore, my testimony in the school was not very powerful, and when I witnessed to Brother Weigh he paid no heed.

After becoming a Christian I had spontaneously a desire to bring others to Christ, but after a year of witnessing and bearing testimony to my schoolmates there was no visible result. I thought that more words and more reasons would be effective, but my testimony did not seem to have a powerful effect on others. Some time later I met a Western missionary, Miss Grose, who asked me how many persons had been saved through me during that first year. I bowed my head and shamefully confessed that despite my attempts to preach the gospel to my schoolmates, no one had responded. She said to me frankly that there was something between the Lord and me hindering my effectiveness. Perhaps it was hidden sin, or debts, or some such matter. I admitted that such things did exist. She asked me if I were willing to settle them straight away. I agreed. Then she asked me how I made my witness, and I told her that I chose people at random and spoke to them about the Lord regardless of whether they showed any interest. At this she replied that I ought rather to make a list and pray for my friends first, then wait for God's opportunity to talk to them.

Immediately I started putting right the matters that were hindering my effectiveness, and also made a list of seventy friends to pray for daily. Some days I would pray for them every hour, even in class. When the opportunity came I would try to persuade them to believe in the Lord Jesus. My schoolmates often said jokingly, "Mr. Preacher is coming. Let's listen to his preaching," although in fact they had no intention of listening. I reported my failure to Sister Grose and she persuaded me to continue praying until some were saved. With the Lord's grace I continued to pray daily, and after several months all but one of the seventy persons were saved. [1]

———————————◆———————————

Watchman Nee's experience of finding Christ took place when he was a successful young man. He was intelligent. He was promising. He had dreams and plans that he felt confident he could achieve. Apparently, he didn't need Christ. Perhaps this is similar to your situation. You are doing well and seem to be quite self-sufficient. But, like Nee, you must realize that Jesus Christ has a claim on your life.

Christ has a claim on every man's life because man was made in God's image. Genesis 1:27 says, "So God created man in His own image; in the image of God He created him." And the image of God is Christ (2 Cor. 4:4; Col. 1:15). Since you have been made according to

Christ, He has a claim on your life.

Though you may consider your life a success, according to God's thought, success without Christ is failure. The meaning of your life and destiny is wrapped up with Christ. That is why Romans 8:29 says, "For whom He foreknew, He also *predestined* to be conformed to the image of His Son, that He might be the firstborn among many brethren."

You need to settle your destiny at once and receive Christ with the realization that your whole life belongs to Him. When Paul was saved on the Damascus road, he cried out, "Lord, what do You want me to do?" (Acts 9:6). God has a plan for your life, but for that plan to be worked out, you must cooperate by surrendering to Him and allowing Him to *work* in you and *do* in you His good pleasure (Phil. 2:13). Trust Him with your life and you will prove the reality of Ephesians 3:20: "Now unto Him who is able to do exceedingly abundantly above all that we ask or think, according to the power that works in us."

As you take a step of faith to receive Christ, you will find that God's power will automatically do in you what you could not do in yourself. You will be like Abraham, who was "strong in faith, giving glory to God; and being fully persuaded that, what He had promised, He was able also to perform" (Rom. 4:20-21). Just as Watchman Nee testified, you too will be able to say, "Oh Lord, You have indeed been gracious to me."

17 The Assurance that You Have Found Christ

THE MOST BASIC thing in your relationship with God is to have the assurance that Jesus Christ lives in you. The Bible guarantees that you can have this assurance:

> *"God was pleased to reveal **His Son in me**."*
>
> Galatians 1:15-16

> *"Behold, I [Christ] stand at the door and knock; if any one hears My voice and opens the door, **I will come into him**."*
>
> Revelation 3:20

> *"Do you not recognize this about yourselves, that **Jesus Christ is in you** . . . ?"* 2 Corinthians 13:5

> *"God willed to make known what is the riches of the glory of this mystery among the Gentiles, which is **Christ in you, the hope of glory**."* Colossians 1:27

> *"If **Christ is in you** . . . the spirit is life because of righteousness."*
>
> Romans 8:10

Since the Bible reveals that man can have the definite assurance that Christ lives in him, how do you personally gain this assurance?

1 THE FIRST STEP in gaining the assurance that Jesus Christ lives in you is to **understand** that man was created with an inner capacity for Christ to live in him. The Bible describes this capacity by telling us that man is composed of three parts:

> *"Now may the God of peace Himself sanctify you entirely; and may your* ***spirit*** *and* ***soul*** *and* ***body*** *be preserved complete, without blame at the coming of our Lord Jesus Christ."*
> 1 Thessalonians 5:23

The human spirit is the place in man where Christ comes to live:

> *"The Lord who . . . forms* ***the spirit of man*** *within him."*
> Zechariah 12:1

> *"The one who joins himself to the Lord is* ***one spirit*** *with Him."*   1 Corinthians 6:17

> *"That which is born of the Spirit is* ***spirit.****"*   John 3:6

> *"The Lord Jesus Christ be with* ***your spirit.****"*
> 2 Timothy 4:22

When you receive Christ, He enters directly into your spirit and you are born again.

2 THE SECOND STEP in gaining the assurance that Christ lives in you is to **acknowledge** man's problem of sin in the light of God's Word. The Bible diagnoses the condition of every man before God:

*"And you, being **dead in your trespasses and sins** . . ."*
Ephesians 2:1

*"For **all have sinned** and fall short of the glory of God."*
Romans 3:23

*"**If we say that we have not sinned, we make Him a liar, and His word is not in us.**"*
1 John 1:10

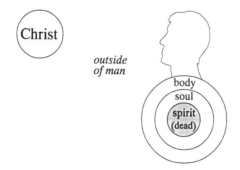

Because of the problem of sin, man is separated from God, and his spirit is dead.

Therefore, man's problem of sin and separation from God must be solved.

3 THE THIRD STEP in gaining the assurance that Christ lives in you is to **believe** that Jesus Christ is the Son of God and has made full provision to live in you.

WHAT JESUS CHRIST HAS DONE
IN ORDER TO COME INTO YOU:

- As God, He was incarnated and became a man.
- As man, He lived a sinless life to be our Savior.
- As our Savior, He died on the cross for our sins.
- He passed through death, burial, resurrection, and ascension in order that He might *forgive us, come into us,* and *indwell us.* This entire process is portrayed in the following diagram:

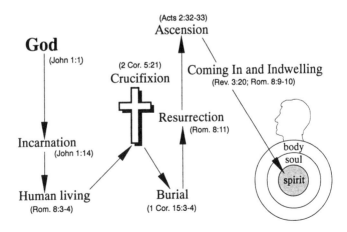

4 THE FINAL STEP in gaining the assurance that Christ lives in you is to **receive** Him. The Bible invites you to receive Jesus Christ. It also gives you the assurance that when you receive Him, He comes into you and you immediately **become** a child of God:

> [12] *"But as many as **received Him**, to them He gave the right to **become children of God**, even to those who believe in His name, [13] who were born not of blood, nor of the will of the flesh, nor of the will of man, but of God."* John 1:12-13

By receiving Christ a change takes place in you. You are born of God. Christ comes in to dwell in your spirit in order that you might enjoy constant fellowship with Him:

*"Behold, **I stand at the door and knock**; if any one hears My voice and opens the door, **I will come into him**, and will dine with him, and he with Me."*

Revelation 3:20

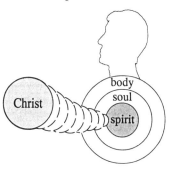

You can now have the full assurance that Jesus Christ lives in you by opening the door of your heart and inviting Him in. The moment you do, **He will come into you.**

HOW TO OPEN AND RECEIVE CHRIST:

1. Confess His Name:

> [9] *"If you confess with your mouth the Lord Jesus and believe in your heart that God has raised Him from the dead, you will be saved;* [10] *for with the heart man believes unto righteousness, and with the mouth confession is made unto salvation."* Romans 10:9-10

2. Simply ask Jesus Christ to come into you.

The following is a suggested prayer to help you open your heart to the Lord and receive Him:

"Lord Jesus, I open myself to You and acknowledge that I am a sinner. I believe that You love me and shed Your blood on the cross for all my sins. I believe in my heart that You were raised from the dead and that You are here right now. I repent of all my sins. I open my heart to You and receive You this moment.

Thank You for coming into me. Thank You for forgiving all my sins. Thank You for this blessed assurance that You live inside of me. I believe that I have become a child of God.

I now turn over my whole life to You. I want You to live in me and be my life. Lord Jesus, I love You. I now confess with my mouth Your precious Name — Lord Jesus! Lord Jesus! Amen!"

THE ASSURANCE THAT CHRIST IS IN YOU

Now that you have prayed and received Christ into you, God wants you to **know** that you have been heard and that Jesus Christ, the Son of God, is now living in you. His Word gives you the assurance that you now have eternal life because you have the Son of God living in you:

> [12] *"**He who has the Son has the life;** he who does not have the Son of God does not have the life.*
>
> [13] *These things **I have written to you** who believe in the name of the Son of God, **in order that you may know that you have eternal life.***
>
> [14] *And this is the confidence which we have toward Him, that, **if we ask anything according to His will, He hears us.***
>
> [15] *And if **we know** that He hears us in whatever we ask, **we know that we have the requests** which we have asked from Him."* 1 John 5:12-15

Your prayer to receive Christ was according to God's will. The Word of God assures you that He has heard you. You have the Son! You have eternal life! You are forgiven! Christ now dwells in your spirit! God's Word gives you the definite assurance that Jesus Christ is now living in you.

Your Name _____

Date _____

Endnotes

Chapter 1 *Aurelius Augustine*

1. J. G. Pilkington, trans., *The Confessions of St. Augustine,* 8.5.10, Nicene and Post-Nicene Fathers, 1st ser., vol. 1 (reprint, Grand Rapids, Mich.: Wm. B. Eerdmans Publishing Co., 1974), pp. 120-121; used in combination with A. C. Outler, trans. & ed., *Augustine: Confessions and Enchiridion,* Library of Christian Classics, vol. 7 (Philadelphia: The Westminster Press, 1955), p. 164.
2. Pilkington, pp. 126-128; Outler, pp. 173-177.
3. F. B. Meyer, *Back to Bethel* (Chicago: Moody Press, 1901), pp. 77-78.
4. Ibid., p. 78.
5. Ambrose, *Concerning Repentance,* 2.10.96, Nicene and Post-Nicene Fathers, 2nd ser., vol. 10 (reprint, Grand Rapids, Mich.: Wm. B. Eerdmans Publishing Co., 1969), p. 357.

Chapter 2 *Martin Luther*

1. Roland H. Bainton, *Here I Stand: A Life of Martin Luther* (Nashville, Tenn.: Abingdon, 1950), p. 54.
2. Ibid., p. 65.
3. Ewald M. Plass, comp., *What Luther Says,* vol. 3 (St. Louis, Mo.: Concordia Publishing House, 1959), pp. 1226-1230.
4. Bainton, op. cit., p. 65.

5. Martin Luther, *A Commentary on St. Paul's Epistle to the Galatians* (Cambridge: James Clarke & Co., 1953), pp. 503-506.

Chapter 3 *John Calvin*

1. John Calvin, *Commentary on the Book of Psalms,* vol. 1, Calvin's Commentaries, vol. 4 (reprint, Grand Rapids, Mich.: Baker Book House, 1993), p. xl.
2. Ibid.
3. Ibid., p. xlii.
4. John Dillenberger, ed., *John Calvin* (Garden City, N.Y.: Doubleday & Co., Anchor Books, 1971), p. 9.
5. Calvin, op. cit., p. xl.
6. John C. Olin, ed., *A Reformation Debate: John Calvin & Jacopo Sadoleto* (1966; reprint, Grand Rapids, Mich.: Baker Book House, 1976), pp. 87-90.
7. Calvin, op. cit., pp. xl-xliv.
8. Ibid., p. xl.

Chapter 4 *John Bunyan*

1. John Bunyan, *Grace Abounding to the Chief of Sinners* (Chicago: Moody Press, 1959), pp. 65-68, 73-75, 79-82; used in combination with John Bunyan, *Grace Abounding to the Chief of Sinners,* The Complete Works of John Bunyan, illustrated ed. (Philadelphia: Bradley, Garretson & Co., 1873), pp. 52-53, 58-59.

Chapter 5   *Madame Guyon*

1. Thomas T. Allen, trans., W. A. Hutchinson, ed., *The Autobiography of Madame Guyon* (New Canaan, Conn.: Keats Publishing, Inc., 1980), pp. 33-34, 39-45; used in combination with Jeanne Marie Bouvier de la Mothe Guyon, *Madame Guyon: An Autobiography* (Chicago: Moody Press, n.d.), pp. 68-72.
2. Thomas C. Upham, *Life of Madame de la Mothe Guyon* (London: Sampson Low, Marston, Searle, and Rivington, 1877), pp. 36-38.
3. Guyon, op. cit., pp. 74-75.
4. Upham, op. cit., pp. 38-39.

Chapter 6   *John Wesley*

1. Nehemiah Curnock, ed., *The Journal of John Wesley,* vol. 1, standard ed. (London: Robert Culley, n.d.), pp. 465-477.
2. Martin Luther, *Martin Luther's Preface to the Epistle to the Romans* (Adelaide, South Australia: Lutheran Publishing House, n.d.), pp. 12-13.

Chapter 7   *Jonathan Edwards*

1. Edward Hickman, ed., *The Works of Jonathan Edwards,* vol. 1 (Carlisle, Pa.: The Banner of Truth Trust, 1974), pp. xii-xiii.

Chapter 8   *George Whitefield*

1. George Whitefield, *Journals of George Whitefield* (Grand Rapids, Mich.: Christian Classics, n.d.), p. 19.
2. Ibid., pp. 17-20.
3. Henry Scougal, *The Life of God in the Soul of Man* (London: InterVarsity Fellowship, 1961), pp. 12-13.

Chapter 9   *Charles Finney*

1. Charles G. Finney, *Memoirs of Rev. Charles G. Finney* (New York: Fleming H. Revell Co., 1903), pp. 12-17.

Chapter 10   *George Müller*

1. G. F. Bergin, comp., *Autobiography of George Müller,* 4th ed. (London: Pickering & Inglis, 1929), pp. 1-10.

Chapter 11   *Andrew Murray*

1. J. Du Plessis, *The Life of Andrew Murray of South Africa* (London: Marshall Brothers, n.d.), pp. 42-43.
2. Ibid., pp. 64-65.
3. Ibid., p. 66.
4. Ibid., pp. 70-71.

Chapter 12   *Hannah Whitall Smith*

1. Hannah Whitall Smith, *The Unselfishness of God* (Used with permission. Published by Barbour Publish-

ing, Inc., P. O. Box 719, Uhrichsville, Ohio 44683), © 1993, pp. 131-139.

Chapter 13   *J. Hudson Taylor*

1. J. Hudson Taylor, *A Retrospect* (Chicago: Moody Press, n.d.), pp. 8-13.

Chapter 14   *Charles Spurgeon*

1. Charles Haddon Spurgeon, *Conversion: the Great Change* (Pasadena, Tex.: Pilgrim Publications, 1977), pp. 15-21.

Chapter 15   *A. B. Simpson*

1. A. E. Thompson, *The Life of A. B. Simpson* (Harrisburg, Pa.: The Christian Alliance Publishing Co., 1920), pp. 11-17.

Chapter 16   *Watchman Nee*

1. K. H. Weigh, comp., *Watchman Nee's Testimony* (Kowloon, Hong Kong: Church Book Room, 1974), pp. 9-14.

inistry
Publications

Other Available Books:
by Bill Freeman

The Supplied Life
A Daily Devotional • 409 pages

Spending Time with the Lord
A practical guide in learning how to spend
time with the Lord • 87 pages

God's Unconditional Love
The nature of God's love revealed
in the book of Hosea • 237 pages

Calling Upon the Name of the Lord
A study of the meaning, history, and basis of calling
upon the Name of the Lord • 149 pages

The Cross and the Self
Fellowship on experiencing the
cross in our daily life • 305 pages

Our Common Oneness
A study in the book of Romans revealing
the oneness of all believers • 284 pages

The Kingdom Life
A study in the book of James showing the nature
of the kingdom life in our daily life • 227 pages

Hearing the Lord's Voice
A study of Scriptures related to hearing
the Lord's voice in our experience • 118 pages

Seeing and Feeling the Church
A study of Paul's prayers in Ephesians • 138 pages

The Church Is Christ
A look into the deep significance
of 1 Corinthians 12:12 • 238 pages

Vision in the Christian Life
The importance of vision in living the
Christian life • 99 pages

The Triune God in Experience
A study of the experiential emphasis on the
Triune God through church history • 391 pages

by Kirk Eland

Christ: the Christian Life
A step-by-step study of the basic truths and
experiences of the Christian life • Especially helpful
for new believers • 218 pages

Y ou may use any of the following ways to obtain books
from *Ministry Publications:*

(1) Available at Christian bookstores everywhere through
   Spring Arbor Distributors
(2) Write: P. O. Box 12222, Scottsdale, AZ 85267 • USA
(3) Phone: (602) 948-4050 / (800) 573-4105
(4) Fax: (602) 922-1338
(5) E-mail: MinWord12@aol.com
(6) Order by web site: http://www.thechristian.org